STARTING OVER
But not from scratch!

STARTING
OVER
But not from scratch!
Spiritual & Mental Health Between Jobs

RICHARD KEW

ABINGDON PRESS
Nashville

STARTING OVER, BUT NOT FROM SCRATCH
SPIRITUAL AND MENTAL HEALTH BETWEEN JOBS

Copyright © 1994 by Abingdon Press

This book is printed on recycled, acid-free paper.

Library of Congress Cataloging-in-Publication Date

Kew, Richard, 1945–
    Starting over–but not from scratch: spiritual and mental health between jobs/Richard Kew.
        p.   cm.
    ISBN 0-687-27702-7 (alk. paper)
    1. Unemployed–Religions life. 2. Job hunting–Religious aspects–Christianity. I. Title
BV4596.U53K48   1994
248.8'8–dc20   93-33343
                                                                                CIP

I have changed many of the names of individuals whose stories I have told to guard their anonymity. In some cases I have also disguised their geographical location. All the incidents described are genuine and factual, but I feel it essential to protect the privacy of the women and men whom I have described, all of whom have since moved on to new chapters of their lives.

Scripture quotations are from the New Revised Standard Version Bible, copyright © 1989 by the Division of Christian Education of the National Council of the Churches of Christ in the USA. Used by Permission.

The author gratefully acknowledges the following for permission to reprint text:

AIO Press, for excerpts from *An Australian Prayer Book.* Copyright Anglican Church of Australia Trust Corporation.

SPCK for all of the following:

    excerpts from *Prayers for Everyone,* by Frank Colquhoun. Copyright © 1991 by SPCK.

    excerpts from *Prayers for Today,* by Frank Colquhoun. Copyright © by SPCK.

    excerpts from *Family Prayers,* by Frank Colquhoun. Copyright © 1984 by SPCK.

    excerpts from *Power Lines,* by David Adam. Copyright © 1992 by SPCK.

94 95 96 97 98 99 00 01 02 03 — 10 9 8 7 6 5 4 3 2 1

MANUFACTURED IN THE UNITED STATES OF AMERICA

I dedicate this book
to my two wonderful daughters,
Olivia and "Lindy,"
each of whom, in her own special way,
has brought her parents great joy and happiness.

CONTENTS

PREFACE

Life is full of surprises!

A serendipitous and unexpected confluence of events about ten years ago resulted in my becoming a regular contributor to the columns of the Dow Jones' employment publication, the *National Business Employment Weekly*.

"We get lots of 'how to' articles about finding jobs," then editor, V. J. Pappas, told me at the beginning of that relationship. "But I think people out of work need something more than that. Do you think you could let us have occasional articles which are more pastoral, about taking care of yourself when you're between jobs?"

So from the mid-1980s onward a steady procession of pieces designed to help people look after themselves emotionally and spiritually through what is usually a most traumatic transition began marching out of my computer. The editors liked them, and, to my surprise, the readers found them helpful. Having an unusual last name and living in a small college town in Tennessee made me easy to track down. This has meant that over the years scores of letters and phone calls have reached me from *National Business Employment Weekly* readers.

With the global economy going through the most traumatic of transitions, and with huge numbers of Americans feeling less secure in their jobs than ever before, my publishers and I realized the time had come to turn those articles into a book to help people through the hard times of employment uncertainty. It was not appropriate in *National Business Employment Weekly,* a secular publication, to spell out the detailed spiritual implications of being out of work, but in this book I am able to make explicit what was merely implicit in previous contributions.

I am grateful to a succession of wonderful people at *National Business Employment Weekly* who helped me to formulate my ideas, corrected my punctuation, and stimulated me to write. I am especially appreciative of V. J. Pappas, the editor of the publication during the 1980s; Tony Lee, its present editor; and his associate, Perri Capell. I'm very enthusiastic about the *National Business Employment Weekly,* and believe it is a vital resource for all professionals who are between jobs.

Then there's Patti Feher, who spent many hours correcting and critiquing the manuscript before I finally delivered it into the hands of the publishers. Not only did she make many valuable suggestions, but she managed to translate my occasional lapses into British English back into language that would be understood by Americans!

Last, but by no means least, I want to thank my wife, Rosemary, whose wisdom and good sense lurk somewhere in most of the chapters I have written. In many ways this book has been a family effort, for it was hammered out on the anvil of job transitions both of us have made, and our pastoral relationships with others who have been going through such periods, and my experience as both a professional and an amateur career counselor.

Some of the many job hunters I have worked with in a one-on-one basis have quoted to me the words of Paul that "in all things God works for the good of those who love him" (see Rom. 8:28). That is true. It is my hope and prayer that this book will help to make this inevitably trying experience one of richness and blessing for you.

Richard Kew

C H A P T E R
ONE

NEW BEGINNINGS

*Lord, since we know not what lies ahead of us in life's journey,
guide our future steps in the way of your will; for in fulfilling
your plan for our lives we shall be doing what is best for us, and
most for your glory.*

Frank Colquhoun

Tony was an upwardly mobile oil engineer in Texas when the
bottom fell out of the world oil market in the mid-1980s.
Responding to a precipitous drop in revenues, his company
hurriedly downsized. Unfortunately, Tony was one of the victims
in the employment bloodbath that followed. Despite all his efforts,
new work was not forthcoming, so it wasn't long before he and his
wife could no longer afford their mortgage. Houses of every kind
just weren't selling in Houston at that time. One morning they
dropped their keys off at the bank and quietly left town.

As agonizing as this experience was, it ultimately brought
Tony and his family to the threshold of a new beginning. While
their lives are not as affluent as they might have once been, today
they are rich with satisfaction. After attending seminary, Tony is
now back in the "oil patch" working as the pastor of a suburban
congregation. I doubt whether he would want to go back to the
"good old days" of conspicuous consumption.

I don't want to sound like a Pollyanna. No one should ever underestimate the miseries of unemployment and the toll it takes on an individual and his or her family. Yet, despite the pain, it is one of the greatest opportunities for growth and change a person can experience. It is not the end of the world. Let me repeat that: *It is not the end of the world!* For most of us, it is a God-given opportunity to start over—make a new beginning. This conviction grew out of personal experience.

My Own Story

When unemployment happened to me, I was like a fish pulled from the water and left flapping around on dry land, gasping for breath. I felt deprived of my dignity and my identity. Overnight, I felt I had been turned into a nobody. Each morning I would watch neighbors set off to their offices, and would have given anything to swap the stress of joblessness for the business worries I knew to be crushing some of them.

For a number of years prior to this turning point in my own life, I had used my skills to help others explore job changes and mid-life crises, or wrestle with unemployment. There is a big difference between helping others and experiencing joblessness yourself! Never in my wildest nightmares did I think this would happen to me. Now I was being forced to come to terms with the distressing reality of being out of work. In my saner moments, I wondered where on earth it would all lead. I had visions of myself lined up for meals at the soup kitchen or selling apples on a street corner.

Like every job searcher I've ever come across, I worried about funds and credit running out. I fretted about the possibility of losing the roof over my head and perhaps worse, being without health care with one of my children falling terribly ill. I would awaken at night in a cold sweat, seized by panic. I would pray fervently that if there was a God somewhere out there (and at times I sincerely doubted it), and if God cared about hurting human beings, he would intervene and bring this horror story to a swift and dramatic conclusion.

While I worried about putting food on my children's plates, an intense inner struggle was shaping up—this was the real drama. Despite my doubts, God was at work; but at the time it didn't feel like it. Stripped of the disguises behind which I had successfully hidden for so long, I was being forced to take a long look at my inner self and resolve some of the long-delayed personal issues that, in the flood, refused to be put off any longer.

Through this dark night of soul and body, I found friends who propped me up and gave me hope. Very often, people I had expected to be most supportive were embarrassed by my plight and shied away. The ones who saw me through into the sunlight at the far end of this dark tunnel into which I had stumbled were an unusual and unexpected array of men and women. They stuck with me through thick and thin, teaching me the true meaning of friendship. Even though I had not been close to some of them before storm clouds gathered over me, they lived out what God's love is all about. They were the ones who were there to rejoice with me when the "right thing" came along and I found my own opportunity to start over.

Unemployment and the Changing World of Work

With the world of work changing so rapidly, unemployment may have lost some of its stigma because it is becoming such a frequent phenomenon. But this does not mean it is any easier to bear. It has always been and will continue to be both draining and, for many, humiliating. Whether or not you are a person of faith won't exempt you from these feelings and experiences. However, let these facts assure you that you aren't down and out or a total deadbeat. Today's college graduates can expect as many as *four* different careers in their working lives and perhaps many more jobs. Those of us who are further down life's road can look forward to perhaps two or three such jolts. Few

Americans can expect to get through without at least one period "between jobs." Joblessness does not mean you are of no use. It means you are being squeezed by the inevitable restructuring of American business and industry as it faces a rougher, tougher, more competitive world.

> *Unemployment has been and will continue to be both draining and, for many, humiliating. Whether or not you are a person of faith won't exempt you from these feelings and experiences.*

In the future, almost no one will be able to boast about working fifty years for the same company and being rewarded with a gold watch and a grateful handshake from the boss at retirement. Such positions are fast diminishing. It is foolish to imagine they will ever come back, so in your job search don't try to go looking for them. Instead of bemoaning this radically altered world, let us strive to view it in positive terms—for then it will open up a whole new array of opportunities to each of us.

Why I Wrote This Book

I've written this book to help you through a tricky transition. This book is designed to be a companion on the puzzling journey you are taking, not just to a new position, but inward into the depths of your heart and soul. Think of it as a soul friend. Despite support from friends, family, and church, the job search is inevitably lonely business. Never forget that God is at your right and your left, directing your path.

Once this ordeal is past, you will be able to look back on it from a safe distance and realize it has been one of the most formative periods of your life—although you may not want to re-experience it anytime soon! This is certainly true of the ex-oil engineer, Tony. He wouldn't trade his new life for his old now that he's crossed the threshold into a different kind of future.

There are times when the unfathomable happens, leaving us frightened and bewildered. It seems to make no sense at the time, yet slowly but surely, a new life starts rising from the ashes of our past like the mythical phoenix. God isn't asleep when bad things happen to us. Instead, God guides us toward a new, richer, and fuller existence. A friend of mine would describe such events as examples of what he calls "God's mischief"—inexplicable at the time they happen, but with the wisdom of hindsight it becomes obvious that all the time the Almighty was in control guiding and directing our lives in new and unexpected ways.

Being thrown out of work is a miserable experience that often turns out to have a silver lining. Many who maneuver their way through the shoals of joblessness find spiritual renewal. They discover that God is real and does come to find them in the depths, where he comforts them. Much to their surprise, they grow in their understanding of themselves and in their knowledge of a loving, caring heavenly Father. Until unemployment shatters their carefully constructed world, many give little thought to either their Creator or their own spiritual needs. As one of their primary security blankets is snatched away they discover that God—the one who seemed to be making mischief—is actually the giver of life.

Let me give you an example of this:

The phone was ringing off the hook when I walked into the house one lunchtime, and I raced to pick it up. "Is that Richard Kew?" the voice asked at the other end of the line. He breathlessly launched into his story.

"I've just read your article in this week's *National Business Employment Weekly,* and I just had to talk to you. I live in New Jersey and lost my job months ago—so far I've found nothing.

It's been a worrying time financially, but for me it has been a fresh start spiritually. I've never been very religious before this; in fact, I hadn't been to church since I graduated from Sunday school years ago. Recently my wife and I have somehow been drawn into the life of the local United Methodist Church. For the first time, I've discovered Jesus Christ is a real person."

It didn't take me long to forget my surprise caller's name, but I will always remember his final words. "You know, Richard, while I wish I had a job again, it's been worth being unemployed so that I could meet the Lord."

This book has been written to help people like my caller and you. It is my profound hope that you and those you love will ultimately gain much from this situation. While there are a few helpful "how to's" on finding work, I am more concerned with providing clues that will enable you to survive the buffeting—and through this experience grow as a person of God. There are plenty of excellent "how-to" books that teach the mechanics of finding work, but I've yet to find one whose primary focus is emotional and spiritual "care and maintenance."

Between the chapters are prayers, devotions, or spiritual resources. When I was without work, there were times when I was so upset with God that I had trouble talking to him, even though I knew I needed him. By using prayers others had written, I was just about able to keep in touch with God. When looking back on those months, I now see how God was reaching out to me and how I was responding with the help of history's prayer writers. This marked a new beginning for my faith.

To get the best out of this book, make liberal use of a highlighter and scribble your comments in the margin. This will help you to re-read any pieces that might have spoken to your needs. If you are married, make a point of sharing this book with your spouse. If you aren't, then be sure you recruit a team of friends who can encourage you along. When the time comes that you need this book no longer, pass it on to others who are beginning this transition to a new life.

Meanwhile—happy hunting. It is my hope and prayer that something wonderful will come out of the travail through which you are now passing. I'm certain this temporary spell will lead to a whole new beginning for you, too!

Help Me, Lord

Help me, Lord, to see
You are about me.
You are my hope.

In my lying down and rising
In my travelling and arriving
Help me, Lord, to see
You are about me.
You are my hope.

In my sorrow and enjoyment
In my work and unemployment
Help me, Lord, to see
You are about me.
You are my hope.

In my health and in my sickness
In my strength and in my weakness
Help me, Lord, to see
You are about me.
You are my hope.

In my peacefulness and strife
In my going from this life
Help me, Lord, to see
You are about me.
You are my hope.

(From *Powerlines,* Celtic prayers about work by David Adam)

C H A P T E R
TWO

FROM THE WHITE HOUSE TO YOUR HOUSE

Life's changes
Dear Lord, through all the changing scenes of life keep my heart
and mind open to the surprises of the Holy Spirit.

Give me your joy in accepting new ways, new thoughts, and
new experiences, so that I may grow in grace to the end of my
days.

Jean Coggan

Rise and Fall

From relatively humble beginnings in the rural South, and amid much fanfare, he reached the pinnacle in his particular field. No sooner had he arrived than things started to go wrong. There he was "in the driver's seat" during uncertain times, and, try as he might, just too many of his problems were due to circumstances utterly beyond his control. Times were hard. He had inherited seemingly intractable difficulties from his predecessors, and progress was further hindered by his own lack of experience. Despite every best effort the work responded slowly and very grudgingly to his ministrations.

Although the dice seemed loaded against him, it came as a nasty shock to learn in November that he would be replaced early in the new year. He found this termination particularly galling—even unfair—because it was his sense that he was beginning to get to the bottom of things. But those who had selected him for the post felt four years were quite enough—if he hadn't succeeded in the time they had allotted, he probably never would.

In many respects, our subject's wife found her husband's severance even more painful. She had shared his aspirations and had worked alongside him as colleague, counselor, and friend for many years. Her determination had been a powerful ingredient in their rise to the top. To her, his termination was not only shortsighted but also cruel. In her more despairing moments she was tempted to lay their demise firmly at God's door.

Yet a further blow awaited them. As the couple prepared to move back to their hometown they were told that an unexpected series of reversals in the family business now threatened their personal financial security. In a matter of weeks it seemed they had been stripped of everything, including position and prestige. When the moving vans came, their life's work lay in tatters around them.

Am I speaking of the demise of the chief executive of a major corporation? Not exactly. The subject of this scenario is President Jimmy Carter following his election defeat in 1980. *Everything to Gain* was the book President Carter and his wife, Rosalyn, wrote several years after he had been swept from office.[1] With candor they describe not just their disappointment and the depression that came in its wake, but also their road back from the slough of despond. For anyone going through a difficult career transition, the Carters' example of Christian faith, fortitude, and creativity, which ultimately transformed defeat into victory, is inspired and timely reading. I commend it to you.

---

1. Jimmy Carter, *Everything to Gain* (New York: Fawcett Books, 1987).

What the Ex-President Can Teach Us

In the years since Jimmy Carter left office, he has won almost universal respect as a champion of peace and the downtrodden. It seems that difficult transition has played a significant role in shaping his extraordinarily productive post-White House years and the work of the Carter Center in Atlanta. There is much each of us can learn from the way the Carters recovered from the blow of rejection.

Losing employment is the experience of tens of thousands of Americans every day. No one is immune—whether one leads the nation or manages the stock room. Coming to terms with the painful realities is no easier for the President of the United States than it is for the butcher, the baker, or the candlestick maker—or the woman who designs computer chips.

Fortunately, most of us are not dependent on an unpredictable electorate for our jobs. But in many instances our departure might be flavored by personality clashes, internal politics, or sheer irrationality, which leave a bitter taste in our mouths. The setback is likely to be as harrowing for you and your family as the loss of the presidency was for the Carters. Fortunately again, unlike them, most of us do not have to live out our grief under the eagle eyes of reporters, television cameras, and an unforgiving public.

The Grieving Process

Losing a job can be as traumatic as losing a loved one. Few newly unemployed people are going to vigorously jump out of bed the day after they've been pink-slipped, eager to face a fresh new morning, however unpleasant the former job might have been. Emotional and spiritual damage has been done, and the healing process takes time. For you the recovery process may be speedy, but be prepared for something that might be rather more drawn out. Many folks are humiliated by joblessness and find themselves waging an agonizing internal war as they attempt to salvage their self-esteem. Expect episodes of grief to creep up on you for weeks, possibly months, to come.

Your plight is bound to *feel* far worse if it is the result of an unjust or mishandled dismissal. This rubs further salt into already festering wounds. More than one ex-worker has said to me, "I feel obsolete and useless; I can't think anyone will look at me ever again." So many people who have said this to me have come back a while later, beaming from ear to ear and ready to launch out into a fresh new opportunity. Unemployment is not the end; it is a new beginning.

When my wife lost a position that had meant a great deal to her, she was as beaten and miserable as I have ever seen her—and we've been married for a quarter of a century. In her case, disbelief at what had happened gave way to depression and anger. It happened in early summer, so she tried to hide from her misery by coaxing the flowers in her garden to grow. Cultivating the soil was a bandage for her wounds. She sought spiritual counsel, and she attempted to pray, but despite all this there were times when it looked as if she would dissolve completely.

During this "in-between time," she had to force herself to keep going. She took a temporary job that hardly satisfied but provided an opportunity to learn new skills and test another area of endeavor. Just as Jimmy Carter used those wilderness years to craft an appropriate job for a former President, so also in the months my wife was recovering from her sense of rejection she was out looking and making herself available. She was good and ready when the perfect opportunity then finally did come along.

If you were fired, then one of your primary tasks during this grieving period is to work out and come to terms with the degree you are responsible for your loss. Most of us find it very difficult to admit we were wrong, that we acted unwisely, or said things that have gotten us into trouble. How much you are prepared to face up to your own shortcomings will affect how you grow emotionally and spiritually as a result of this hiatus in your life.

Are you yet ready to honestly face up to yourself? Perhaps this recovery will involve taking your sins to God for forgiveness through Jesus Christ—maybe your priest or pastor can help you with this part of the process. It is important that you use this interval to come to terms with your own blind spots and shortcomings. We all have them. I've put some prayers at the end of this chapter to help you as you tackle this spiritual side of this equation.

Healing Takes Time

At the front end of my own transition into unemployment I was capable of doing little more than reading novels and watching television for a number of days. I was escaping into myself. Like a hurt animal, I hid away to lick my wounds, wondering if I would ever again want to come out into the light of day. I was listless and lethargic, incapable of doing anything. In actuality, I was mourning all that *might* have been. I was letting go of the dreams and hopes I had cherished. Like poison, they had to be flushed from my system before I was ready to move forward to a new and worthwhile kind of existence. With 20/20 hindsight, I now realize that God's love bore me up through those desert weeks, and then led me out into new and challenging pastures.

From the beginning, make sure you are sharing your plight with caring people who can love you through the present crisis. No one without work should attempt to go it alone.

Convalescence requires a waiting period. If you accidentally cut your finger while preparing the family dinner, you don't expect the wound to miraculously heal itself overnight. So it is with the internal wounds that accompany job loss—you can't see them, but they are likely to be a thousand times deeper. As I've suggested already, the length of time emotional healing takes is different for different people, but the pain will finally go away and you will discover the inner strength to go on to a new beginning. Part of your interior task is to find ways of letting go of the past and preparing for a different kind of future.

The average, emotionally healthy person will probably not take too long to reset the inner compass and again be able to look forward with hope rather than backward in pain. Jimmy Carter rediscovered equilibrium through writing his memoirs, and writing may help you too. In chapter 7 are some suggestions about journals and journaling that you might consider.

From the beginning, make sure you are sharing your plight with caring people who can love you through the present crisis. No one without work should attempt to go it alone. A while back I met a single woman in New Mexico who had been carried through an extended period of unemployment by the women's Bible and prayer group she belonged to. Its members had become real sisters to her, and she always spoke of them with the deepest affection.

Be certain your support group is people who are able to offer "tough love" as well as "warm fuzzies." Sometimes in a job hunt you will need folks around you who are able to prod you along with the proverbial two-by-four, as well as those whose shoulders you can wet with your tears. The best therapy you can get will be a group of people who can critique as well as encourage you as you journey on toward a fresh start.

Questions Galore

During this part of your transition you are letting go of an old set of stresses, while preparing to gird up in preparation for new pressures—those that accompany your job search. Stresses present themselves in different ways, but times of crisis usually come to me with an endless tide of seemingly unanswerable questions:

> How am I going to find something new?
>
> How am I going to fulfill my responsibilities to my family?
>
> What is the bank going to say if I ask them for a loan?
>
> What am I going to tell my parents if everything blows up in my face?
>
> Will this have a terrible impact on my children?
>
> Will the people at church shun me?
>
> Will anyone ever want me again?
>
> Does God really care about me?

Questions are bound to come thick and fast, and unless you are careful in the way you handle them they will further tighten the knots of panic that are tying themselves in the pit of your stomach. It is because of all the questions you are likely to find yourself asking that you will need a good circle of friends and supporters.

Now is the time to turn to whatever relieves your stress and reduces your blood pressure. If you don't have anything to help you take your mind off your problems, then go out and find something. Start building doll houses. Go back to collecting stamps. Chop wood for the winter. Whatever you do, you need something that will help you divert your anxieties and will feed your creativity. I took up writing, and although it hasn't made me rich it certainly has enriched my life both during my period of unemployment and since.

Most of our anxieties are very natural. Some of them call for action as soon as possible. It is vital that you get a clear picture of your financial position and work out ways to meet your obligations over the next few months. This may mean sitting down with a financial adviser, your banker, and your family to work out the details of this process. Even if you don't feel like it, by acting on this very practical issue you will probably jump-start yourself into the job search itself.

This, in turn, may set you to work on updating your résumé and contacting people who can help you as you pull together a network. Each of these activities will inevitably play a part in resetting that internal compass toward the future and away from an unhealthy dwelling upon the past. As you take each step toward a full-fledged job search, another facet of that search will come into view, demanding attention and action on your part.

If you are going to get over the sense of rejection, perhaps the misery that results from the death of treasured ambitions, you need *to allow yourself to feel bad* for a time. *But you can't allow it to go on forever.* You might have failed yourself, but God hasn't let you down. How you feel is both natural and correct. However, while it is important to accept the reality of your pain and to come to terms with it, don't allow yourself to drown in it.

Some Actions You Might Take

Try to avoid being completely immobilized. If you have family responsibilities, volunteer activities, are a Sunday school teacher, or take meals to elderly shut-ins, work hard to throw yourself into these things. Volunteer jobs can certainly help take your mind off your worries. While it might initially take a tremendous effort to go out and face other people, extracurricular responsibilities can be wonderful therapy at times like this. You may not enjoy doing too many of them at first. But if you give them a chance they will moderate the discomforts of your soul when you find yourself tuning into negative messages such as *I can't go on. I'm useless. No one will ever want me again.*

Back to Mr. Carter

Jimmy Carter had to continue as president for eleven weeks after the electorate dismissed him. He had to work with the incoming Republican administration, manage domestic and foreign affairs, wrestle with the economy, and attempt to resolve the seemingly intractable problem of the hostages held in Iran. We ought to be thankful for our own responsibilities, although grateful they don't make these kinds of demands on us, while we are trying to grieve over our broken dreams.

It is easy when you are up against it to think of no one but yourself, and like almost everyone I plead guilty to this "sin." Yet, the less-regimented structure to our days during career transition provides time for others. If you aren't involved in volunteer work already, now is the time to begin. There is nothing more salutary than time set aside for those less fortunate than ourselves—especially when we perceive ourselves as victims. Commit to volunteer work, and you will find courage in unexpected places. This will recharge your internal batteries—remember, the Carters went off to work for Habitat for Humanity, building houses for low-income families.

If you already belong to a church, your pastor or priest will probably be able to find 101 things for you to do. Churches and most charitable organizations usually have more tasks to do than hands to perform them. Perhaps you have some particular skill that one of these organizations could really use. On the other hand, you could discover yourself learning new skills that might be put to use when you find your new position. More than this, I think I can promise that you will meet new people and find yourself adding valuable names to your network.

Most of us do not realize how much we take for granted the right to work until it is taken away from us. Honest, demanding work gives self-esteem, a sense of dignity, and an opportunity to contribute to the good of the community. The Lord God set Adam to work in the Garden of Eden at the beginning of Genesis, so it is not surprising that as his daughters and sons our need to work comes to us naturally. We were created to earn an honest living with our brains and the sweat of our brow.

We began this chapter with Jimmy Carter, so perhaps we should end with him. When he left the White House he was a beaten man. He would have become one of the pathetic failures of American history if he had sloped off to Plains, Georgia, and spent the rest of his life licking his wounds, wondering "What if. . . ?" But he did not. Once he had recovered from the shock, he set to work building a new career that has made the world a better place to live in.

Although history may eventually judge Mr. Carter as president more generously than it does now, he will certainly go down as one of the greatest ex-presidents. Indeed, it has been said that Jimmy Carter has set the benchmark against which his successors will be measured. The lesson for each of us is that there is life after job loss. However hard or humiliating it might have been, God probably still has substantial things for each of us to do—our task is to go out and find them!

Myself
My Father, thank you for knowing me better than I know myself.

Thank you for letting me know myself better than others know me.

Make me better than they suppose I am, and forgive me for what they do not know. For Jesus Christ's sake.
(Based on an Islamic prayer)

Lord God, I recognise the truth of the saying that "I am not what I think I am, but what I *think*, I am."

My thoughts shape my character and personality and

determine what I say and do.

By your grace then I will guard my thoughts and drive out the false and evil ones by letting in those that are true and good.

So may I be the person *you* want me to be, and not what I think I am.

Our character

Our Father, help us to remember that what we are matters more than what we do, and that our character is the only thing we shall take out of this world when we die.

Make us the sort of people you want us to be.

Direct our thoughts, our interests, our ambitions, that we may build a sound Christian character on the foundations of love, kindness, honesty, truthfulness and faith; that apart from our words and actions, what we are may be a witness to him whom we love and serve, Jesus Christ our Lord.

THREE

CRISIS AS OPPORTUNITY

For ourselves
Fix thou our steps, O Lord, that we stagger not at the uneven
motions of the world, but steadily go on to our glorious home;
neither censuring our journey by the weather we meet with, nor
turning out of the way for anything that befalls us. The winds are
often rough, and our own weight presses us downwards.

Reach forth, O Lord, thy hand, thy saving hand, and speedily
deliver us.

John Wesley

A Lesson the Chinese Can Teach Us

The new direction Jimmy and Rosalyn Carter's lives took after such a major disappointment and setback is just one piece of evidence that crisis and opportunity can in reality be turned into the opposite sides of the same coin. This was something the Chinese discovered centuries ago. They noticed that every cloud really does have a silver lining, and so they built this startling observation into their language. The pictograph of their complicated alphabet that symbolizes *crisis* can also be interpreted to mean both *danger* and *opportunity.* They recognized that although crises might stir up terrible anxieties deep inside us, if we handle them wisely the disruptions they cause can be turned into the raw material for a brand-new beginning, a chance to start over.

Whether we like it or not, most of us very easily tend to get set in our ways. Often it takes one almighty crisis to jump us out of the ruts into which our lives have slipped. Crises by their very nature force us to take a long, cool look at ourselves, then make the necessary, but vital, adjustments—these may turn out to be quite radical. At turning points like this we might come face to face with our God as never before. This can be quite a surprise to those who for years might have considered the divine a total irrelevance. But more about that in a later chapter.

From where you're sitting now, what you are passing through probably feels like hell. But I don't want you to be too discouraged. As uncomfortable as this episode feels, it could turn out to be one of the most fruitful periods of your life—a genuine emotional and spiritual crossroad. If you mope and allow yourself to turn in on yourself, a great opportunity could well be lost. Handled constructively, this transition will not only renovate you but will steer you in the direction of a brand-new career. Perhaps you will discover talents you didn't know you possessed!

Some years ago a gifted former currency broker came to see me. "Trading money," he told me as he described its intricacies, "is a young man's game. I guess I'm getting too long in the tooth for it. I started losing my cool, my nerve, and my judgment." He was a sad and dejected figure, made more pitiful by the little razor cut on his chin and the coffee stain in the middle of his tie. My heart went out to him as he sat there in my office.

James had been out of work for many months. He and his wife had been forced to sell their lovely home in an expensive New York suburb to move with their children to cheaper accommodations Upstate. Here they depended on her income as a secretary to keep them afloat, although he had been able to pick up a little freelance bookkeeping. Such circumstances were, obviously, very discouraging, but instead of trying to see this as an opportunity for a fresh start, and to position himself accordingly, my friend viewed everything through the fog of what he perceived to be failure. I was never able to help him over this hurdle. He was hurt and humiliated, and seemed determined to stay that way. I lost touch with this gifted guy, so I did not discover whether he found something to make the second half of his working life sparkle as the first had. He was a very able person, and it grieved me to see him wasting his life.

Crisis-Risk-Opportunity

Like James, some people who lose their jobs use the unpleasantness of the experience to feed their misery. But feeling permanently sorry for yourself or mad at your former employer is not only emotionally crippling, but will hamper your job search as well. Whether it was your fault or not that the position dissolved, once the first throes of grief are over, it is vital that you make every effort to close the door on the past and prepare for a new and productive future.

Marianne was in public relations with a large nonprofit company based in a major city. She loved her work, but like so many working mothers was forced to juggle family responsibilities and career to hold down her job. Then downsizing began, and to everyone's horror, her position was eliminated. Her friends gathered around and encouraged her through months of what seemed like fruitless searching in a very tight job market. Once she had gotten over the shock of losing her job, she worked hard at it, not allowing past distresses to cloud her vision.

Finally, she landed a new position. Public relations and some earlier experience as a journalist had developed a cross section of skills that were perfect for a brand-new career—this one in publishing. She would not have left the comfort of her former position if restructuring had not taken place. Without that distressing crisis, she would have missed exciting new challenges and opportunities.

New beginnings are fresh green shoots that push through the soil of rejection and discomfort, then blossom impressively. To change the metaphor, making a fresh start is like giving birth, agonizing labor pains being a necessary part of the birthing process. Tears of anguish quickly turn to joy when the child is born. So it is when the job search ends and you find yourself employed again.

Job Hunter as Creator

As you read this heading you might have wondered if there is anything creative about job hunting at all. From where you find yourself at the moment, it probably seems like an endless round of presenting yourself to a world that at this point doesn't seem very interested in what you have to offer. If you're thinking like this, then you are dead wrong.

A well-run career search makes greater demands on our reservoirs of creativity and initiative than most jobs ever will, but most of us have more creativity than we realize. Crises have the knack of levering the lid off the strongbox in which we store it all away. The secret of success is making sure the lid is not put back on that box when the job search is over.

Imagine yourself as an artist. Before you is a canvas and in your hand a palette of colors. Your task is to transform these simple ingredients into a thing of beauty—a picture you are proud to hang on your wall or give to a friend. Certainly there are risks when painting. You might make false starts, even messing up a canvas or two, but sitting in a corner bemoaning your lack of skill is no excuse for not trying.

Winston Churchill was a middle-aged government official in World War I, facing a terrifying situation. One weekend, desperate to ameliorate his anxieties, he borrowed some paints and started daubing colors on a canvas. His initial tries were hardly masterpieces, but he persevered and eventually became almost as accomplished an amateur painter as he was a skilled professional politician.

You may never have had to go out looking for work before, but like Churchill, all of us have within ourselves deep springs of God-given creativity—most of which have never been tapped. Right now your assignment is to discover and channel them into the serious business of finding satisfying employment. But don't let them slip from your grasp when the search is over. You will need them in almost anything you'll do in the years ahead.

Of the hundreds of people I have watched go out searching for a new beginning, the ones who have done best in the long run have been those who have combined dogged persistence with the best of their imagination. I have to admire one middle-aged woman I saw on CBS's "Sixty Minutes." She had once been a doyen of Beverly Hills society but had fallen on hard times. Somehow she had used her creativity to persuade the network to put her on the program in her attempt to land work in television. I do not know whether she succeeded, but she gets high marks for ingenuity!

All of us have within ourselves deep springs of God-given creativity — most of which have never been tapped. Right now your assignment is to discover them. But don't let them slip from your grasp when the search is over. You will need them in almost anything you'll do in the years ahead.

Anyone can put a hundred letters and résumés into the mail and then sit back waiting for the world to beat a path to the door. These people will be disappointed. Employers aren't looking for passive, uninventive people. Folks who handle a job search unimaginatively will be palmed off with those bland form letters most potential employers have stored in their computers to cover such eventualities. Some don't even bother to reply at all.

Today's corporations, both large and small, need women and men who are not only self-starters, but who bring enthusiasm and creativity, as well as professional skills and qualifications. Demonstrate these qualities in your search, and immediately you will stand out from the crowd. Not only will you get interviews, but you will eventually land a position that both challenges and satisfies. Delve deep inside and discover some of your God-given gifts of imagination and creativity!

Thinking Critically About Yourself

Creative job hunters should be prepared to go through the difficult exercise of *thinking critically about themselves.* Most of us find this an unpleasant assignment even at the best of times, but it requires considerable effort when things are going badly. It is essential if you are to get a fix on what you have to offer—as well as your shortcomings. In a job search, temptations tend to come from both ends of the spectrum: Either we overvalue our strengths and play down our weaknesses, or we consider ourselves miserable worms and cripple our self-esteem.

When you undertake a job hunt it is important that you try to be as objective about yourself as possible. Getting yourself into perspective can be a fruitful, if sometimes painful, exercise whose benefits will transform every aspect of the rest of your life. It is not something most of us do well alone. You *must* find someone to help you.

At a crucial moment in my own search I sought the help of a career counselor. I was lonely and disillusioned. I entered his office thinking I was useless, but within a few weeks was overwhelmed by the possibilities! Counseling is expensive, and I have to warn you that it took me months to pay my debts. But I don't regret a penny of it! If a career counselor is beyond your means, seek the advice of your pastor. He or she might be of help or be able to put you in touch with someone at the church who will guide you through this process.

Looking for new work is an exercise in *marketing*. Successful salespersons believe in the products they are attempting to sell. Most of us tend not to believe the salesperson who gives the impression that a product is perfect. One of the reasons I bought the car I drive was that after having praised its strengths, the salesman made sure I was aware of its shortcomings. With over 100,000 miles on the odometer I'm still happy with my decision of some six years ago.

When you are interviewed, your having a grasp of your weaknesses as well as your strengths is vital. Many a canny interviewer will ask you to describe your various Achilles' heels. Knowing where you are likely to stumble will help you to present yourself to a potential employer in a way that is both honest and demonstrative of your possessing genuine personal integrity. If you have learned how to be creatively critical of yourself, you will know that in addition to your shortcomings, you have a tremendous amount more to offer any employer with the perspicacity to hire you!

People who know themselves well are an enormous asset to any organization, and they will be increasingly so in years to come. They also carry this over into every other aspect of their daily life. Spiritual and emotional growth depend on our being honest about ourselves in the eyes of God.

Personal Responsibility

Job hunts are occasions *par excellence* when we must take responsibility for our own lives. No one else is able to prepare a résumé for us, neither are there stand-ins who will make the contacts and the calls that are the lifeblood of a fruitful campaign. Ingenuity will be required if you are to develop a network, set up exploratory interviews, identify good contacts, and eventually bring your search to a successful conclusion.

There always needs to be people around to provide support and advice and shoulders to cry on when things are going badly. But we have to do the footwork ourselves if we are to open the doors that will lead us toward a new beginning.

Perhaps one of the hardest facets of being personally responsible is owning our faults and failures, especially those that are work related. Apart from lay offs, where some impersonal formula has been applied across the board, there is always a tangle of reasons why a person might be out of work.

You might be on the job market now because of clashes over policy or personality or some horrendous, but innocent, mistake. You may have lost your position because you were unable to learn the skills necessary to a rapidly changing workplace, or you just did not fit in that environment. My brother-in-law saw his position evaporate a couple of years ago when he walked into the office one Monday morning to discover that his partners had absconded with all the company's assets, legally compromising him and making him look a terrible fool.

You may have good reason to be angry with your former boss, but a question that needs to be asked and answered honestly is this: What part did you play in your own downfall? One of the ugliest aspects of American life today is the increasing unwillingness of so many of us to bear responsibility for our own actions. Once we are able to accept that we probably contributed to our own workplace demise, we are well on the way to not only inner healing but also new employment.

The eternal password to that new beginning is the word *forgive*. When we can start by forgiving ourselves for our own mistakes, then we will go on to forgive others who might have hurt us. In doing so, we have probably taken the first step down the road of personal and spiritual growth. Forgiveness begins in the heart of God, so I've also put at the end of this chapter some prayers seeking and offering forgiveness that you might find helpful. In some churches there is a form of personal confession to a priest that many find helpful. But if this is not "you," then I am sure your own pastor will have a way of helping you discover the power of God to clear the decks, forgive, and make a fresh start.

I left one of my former positions under a cloud. At first I blamed my failure on everyone but myself, but in my heart of hearts I knew from the start that I was as much to blame as those with whom I had worked. Once I had come to terms with this, my feet quickly passed out of the swamp and onto dry ground. It took me quite a time to accept the fact that if in Christ God had forgiven me for my own faults, then I ought to forgive those whom I felt had hurt and misused me. Doing these things enabled me to grow up far more than would have been possible if nothing had ever gone wrong.

Crafting a Network

The most successful job searches depend on a network of individuals able to give good advice, keep their eyes and ears open for the job hunter, and put you in touch with others who can also help. One of your main tasks is to feed and nurture this network because these persons are likely to be your primary contacts that will eventually lead you to a new position. It can be difficult to open up to others about your unemployment, but it is critical that you share your situation so the network can begin to function. A network operates on the principle that the best advertising is by "word of mouth." Someone who knows you is more likely to look out for your interests than the impersonal hit-and-miss business of want ads will allow. You need a network that will keep its eyes open and, when appropriate, suggest your name to potential employers. You are looking for women and men who will get on the phone and say, "Friend, I'd get in touch with Acme Systems if I were you. I think there's a possibility there that you should follow up. Oh, and by the way, I've mentioned your name to them."

It is courteous to thank the folks in your network when they help, and to keep them regularly informed of the progress you are making. Thank-you notes are vital, and perhaps a monthly form letter that you can personalize on your computer is a good way of doing this.

Former President George Bush probably knew more about nurturing a network than anyone in America—one biographer believes he networked his way to the presidency! The Bushes had 30,000 names on their Christmas card list, and Mr. Bush is said to have written ten or twelve thank-you notes a day to people he met on his travels. I'm not suggesting you emulate him, but he has something to teach us all. The more people you effectively incorporate into your search efforts, the more likely you are to be put on the trail of good opportunities.

Risks and Opportunities

Many entertain the misapprehension that to survive this crisis you need plenty of friends, good connections, exceptional gifts and skills, and substantial financial resources. While these will often make the transition easier, survival and growth depend on *you* and the choices you make.

Opportunity and risk go hand in hand. There are risks associated with all the suggestions I've made, but you won't get anywhere unless you are prepared to take the first step on this journey of discovery. In a job hunt, you take your life into your own hands. But even if you feel isolated, you *are* not alone. You have friends; you have family; you have your network. Above all, you have the Lord God Almighty. His presence may not be obvious all the time, but he is the great Leader and Guide.

William Temple, who was England's Archbishop of Canterbury during World War II, once noted that coincidences tended to stop happening when he stopped praying. A good job campaign depends on coincidences and serendipity, and these things will be there a-plenty as God shares this journey with you, and as you share it with God through your prayers.

John is an Episcopal priest who works in New York. Once when I was in the pits of despair and was feeling sorry for myself I complained to him that my life had always been totally devoid of luck—an exaggeration, to be sure, but that was the way I felt. After coaxing out of me what I meant by *luck*, he sat silently for a moment and then answered softly, "People make their own luck, you know."

I spluttered and argued, but I knew he was right. You have the opportunity, in fellowship with God, to make your own luck as you search for your fresh start. There may be times when you think you are near the end of your tether; then all of a sudden whole new vistas will open up. Our God has much to teach us and much to give to us, in times like these.

> Have mercy on me, O God, according to your loving-
> kindness;
> in your great compassion blot out my offenses.
> Wash me through and through from my wickedness,
> and cleanse me from my sins.
> For I know my transgressions only too well,
> and my sin is ever before me.
>
> Holy God, Holy and Mighty, Holy Immortal One,
> have mercy on me.
> (From the Reconciliation of a Penitent, *Book of Common Prayer*, p. 449)

> Almighty and most merciful Father,
> we have strayed from your ways like lost sheep.
> We have left undone what we ought to have done,
> and we have done what we ought not to have done.
> We have followed our own ways and the desires of our own
> hearts.

We have broken your holy laws.
Yet, good Lord, have mercy on us;
restore those who are penitent,
according to your promises declared to mankind in Jesus
    Christ our Lord.
And grant, merciful Father, for his sake,
that we may live a godly and obedient life,
to the glory of your holy name. Amen.
(The General Confession from the *Australian Prayer Book,*
p. 20)

Most merciful God,
we confess that we have sinned against you
in thought, word, and deed,
by what we have done,
and by what we have left undone.
We have not loved you with our whole heart;
we have not loved our neighbors as ourselves.
We are truly sorry and we humbly repent.
For the sake of your Son Jesus Christ,
have mercy on us and forgive us;
that we may delight in your will
and walk in your ways,
to the glory of your Name. Amen.
(The General Confession, Rite II, *Book of Common Prayer,*
p. 79)

C H A P T E R
FOUR

CHANGE, CHANGE, CHANGE

God grant me the serenity
to accept the things I cannot change,
the courage to change the things I can,
and the wisdom to know the difference.

My father spent his whole professional life in the construction industry. Until he retired in the mid-1970s, he had spent most of that time managing the family building business, which he had inherited from his father, in the small English town where I grew up. His strong right hand was a man a few years older than himself who was named Arnold Halsey. Arnold had joined the firm when he was fourteen as my grandfather's office boy. He began by running errands and making the tea, but throughout this apprenticeship he picked up the "trade" he was to ply for the rest of his working life. Changes in construction were so gradual in those days that skills acquired in the 1920s stood him in good stead until he retired some fifty years later, requiring only occasional modest upgrading.

But change has been speeding up, so that in the 1990s things are radically different. Not only has technology transformed construction, but also the whole way the industry is organized nationally and internationally has been altered beyond recognition in just a generation. Poor Arnold would hardly know where to begin today! Apart from the basic assumption that the primary job is to erect buildings, there are few facets of the business that resemble much he would remember. In addition, methods are changing so fast in construction that some skills that might have been state-of-the-art a decade ago already seem prehistoric.

What is true of construction is true of every other kind of work. In some ways, this ever-changing world is an exciting kaleidoscope filled with endless opportunities, but to most of us, it can also be frightening, especially if we are at a crossroad in our lives. Those of us who have been at work for a long time are not used to the fast pace of change. We are likely to respond to things more like dear old Arnold than as members of the fast-moving kind of work force that will be necessary if America is to remain competitive in the brash new century that is hurtling toward us.

The mental image of a lifetime spent in a single career with which many of us grew up is now either extinct or well on its way to sharing the same fate of the dodo or the dinosaur. Concepts learned at our mother's knee about our life's work take a long time to die, but die they must.

Perhaps we have cherished the notion that our working lives would be like that of previous generations—only better. Maybe we envisioned a steady progression forward, skills picked up in college or during those first years on the job being the foundation upon which we would build the rest of our lives. No doubt we said to ourselves, "That's the way it was with good old Dad. Why shouldn't it be like that for me?"

We looked forward to reaching that point on the professional totem pole when we would have almost total job security. With seniority we believed there would be a time when there would be reciprocal loyalty between employer and employee—especially in larger businesses. None of these things is going to happen because of the seismic changes shaking the world of work. Business structures have altered so radically that perhaps the sort of job we were preening ourselves for no longer exists.

In the light of the upheavals of these eruptions in the job market, and the uncertainties they have produced, many of us long to go back to a simpler time rather than being "laboratory specimens" for this brave new world. Unfortunately, you cannot push back the hands of this clock. The world of work is never going to be the same again.

Karl's Story

In the early 1980s, I lived in Rochester, New York. That snowy city on the shores of Lake Ontario is the home of Eastman Kodak, the birthplace of Xerox, and in the eighties was one of the more prosperous high-tech manufacturing centers in the United States. Amazingly, during the few years we lived there whole industries rebuilt themselves, while brand-new ones came into being. New careers burgeoned, while skills that had once been highly regarded withered away. One profession that went into precipitative decline was mechanical engineering.

This group of (mostly) men had been the toast of the town not many years earlier, able to command high salaries and respect. Yet as these extraordinary changes took place, they had less and less to offer. Industry moved forward, but many of these gifted individuals failed to read the writing on the wall. Then suddenly at an unenviable age, they found themselves out on the sidewalk looking for work. Their résumés, which had once been considered impressive, were now catalogues of obsolescent skills. This group of people always springs to mind when I hear those two words many Americans have come to dread: *downsizing* and *restructuring*.

At that time, Karl, a fresh-faced young graduate in mechanical engineering from General Motors Institute, together with his wife, joined the congregation I then pastored. He had shrewdly seen what was happening as soon as he arrived in Rochester to work at a large auto industry component manufacturer. Instead of making the same mistake as older men in his field, he set out to master electronics and complex computer technology, skills he realized the company would need more of in the future—especially if joined with a firm grounding in mechanical disciplines. Not only did he soon find himself involved in a series of fascinating projects, but by his foresight, he guaranteed his job, at least for a few years.

No one can rest on her or his laurels these days, not even a Nobel laureate! Today the disciplinary half-life of an engineer is not much more than five years, and the field is altering with accelerating rapidly. If Karl is to stay in work until he reaches retirement age, he will have to keep ahead of the curve and continue his education for the rest of his active life. What is true of engineering is true in different ways of almost every other professional or workplace skill.

To make themselves attractive to employers, all workers at all levels will need to be permanent students from here on out. Perhaps this spell between jobs that you are now experiencing is a time when you can begin charting the sort of educational course you should follow well into the future, not just for a few months or even a year or two ahead. If you are to succeed in today's workplace, you will have to be involved in learning for the rest of your working life.

Don't think you are too old for the education game. I have a friend who recently went back to school at the age of fifty-five to learn a whole new profession. In years to come he certainly won't be the only gray-hair sitting at the back of the class. I would be surprised if a generation from now colleges and universities are not primarily considered the preserve of the young; they will become increasingly intergenerational places. Listen to what John Naisbitt and Patricia Aburdene have to say: "Like it or not, the information society has turned all of us into lifelong learners who must periodically upgrade our marketable skills and expand our capacity for knowledge."[1]

---

1. John Naisbitt and Patricia Aburdene, *Re-Inventing the Corporation* (New York: Warner Books, 1985), p. 165.

A New Career Path

Those who are still in work, as well as those who are unemployed, ought to give considerable thought to the kind of shape
our working life is likely to have in the future. All of us will go through several significant career changes. In addition, fewer of us will *choose* an early retirement.

Tomorrow's typical career will not have the continuity it might have had in the past; neither will the ideal career path remotely resemble a pleasing upward progression. From now on you are more likely to advance in a zigzag fashion. There will be times when you will be working in a small organization or on your own, then at other times you will either directly or indirectly be part of a large corporation or network of organizations.

> *However your career is structured from now on, if you are to succeed—and I cannot repeat this too often—your career should be marked by a perpetual pursuit of education.*

Your progress will be unusual if it is not punctuated by periods without regular employment—maybe not dissimilar from your present experience. In those times you will possibly find yourself subcontracting your skills to someone, and conceivably you might decide to stay a subcontractor for the remainder of your working life. More and more persons who were once middle managers are discovering in mid-life that if they are to survive they must learn how to turn themselves into self-employed entrepreneurs, selling their abilities to persons or corporations who might need them for a limited time.

However your career is structured from now on, if you are to succeed—and I cannot repeat this too often—your career should be marked by a perpetual pursuit of education. "Those who prepare themselves for change and growth will have the highest probability of success."[2] Remember Karl, the mechanical-turned-electronic engineer? He's the kind of person who will have transferable skills as the shape of the world of work continually alters with frightening swiftness. I expect Karl will always upgrade his education to respond to the changing needs of the market.

Not long ago, one of the major automobile manufacturers purchased land in rural Tennessee near my present home, with a view to eventually building an engine plant. There was much excitement about all those high-paying jobs coming into what has traditionally been a low-wage area. Many dreams were shattered when the president of the car company came and fielded questions at a packed town meeting. That evening he made it clear that very few positions would be open to local people because of inadequate educational levels in the whole region. Most folks don't seem to realize that even traditional "factory floor" positions require the level of math necessary for the worker to handle ever-advancing robotics.

Your Career Is a Vocation

One of the most helpful ways to look at your working life in this radically altered environment is to think of it more as a vocation than as a career. Our word *vocation* comes from the Latin word *vocare,* which means "to call." Some people are frightened by the word *vocation* because they have a tendency to think the only people who have a calling are pastors, priests, missionaries, monks, and nuns. My father understood the term *vocation* more broadly, including teachers, doctors, and lawyers. Even this definition isn't wide enough, because no matter what

---

2. Tom Horton, former CEO, American Management Association, quoted by Tom Peters in *Liberation Management* (New York: Alfred E. Knopf, 1992).

our skills or our background, each of us has been called, and therefore has a vocation.

It is God who has called every Christian into his family—the church—and for each of us God has a unique and special plan. Whatever our education, training, or career history, it is important that we think of ourselves as individuals who have been personally invited by the Lord to be part of his divine household. He then commissions us to ply our own special set of ever-developing skills, and to continue to perfect and upgrade them so that we can be of ongoing use in the fast-changing workplace.

Recognizing that we are where we are because God has put us there gives our lives a sense of purpose. It also provides a genuine cohesion in what promises to be much chopping and changing in the years ahead, as the world tries to find better ways of organizing work. As we've noted, most people are going to find future employment fragmented and, as a result, frustrating. I am certain that if we come to understand that God has called us to be workers in the world's marketplace, then our discomfort will be minimized.

Thinking of our working life as a vocation is appropriate for Christians because it correctly asserts that God calls us to be his servants in the world, and then directs us toward a particular task in a particular setting for a particular period of time. In the past, we have tended to think that once called to do something, then we will do that same thing for a lifetime. Today, nothing could be further from the truth. Instead, we seem to be called to a particular task for a chapter of our lives, from a few months to a number of years. Then God moves us on to something else.

But no matter how many chapters there are, thinking of your working life as a vocation affirms your uniqueness in the sight of God. In each chapter of your life, whether it seems to be a fast-moving progress forward or a discouraging standstill like the present, you are under God's care and protection. By seeing yourself as the practitioner of a calling, when you move from place to place you will begin to recognize ways in which God guides you, nudging you in the direction you are to go. This will add an extraordinary sense of purpose to what might otherwise appear to be a strange jumble of events and activities.

The zigzag kind of career path I've already spelled out might appear frustrating at this stage in your life, more like an obstacle course fraught with danger than a pathway to opportunity. But if you can recognize that God has gifted you in certain ways and has a special place for you, to which he will guide you, then even setbacks during this awkward time of transition will eventually slip into focus. Again and again I have discovered that God wastes none of the experiences he gives us. Even dark moments like this one are rendered meaningful. You will discover that they add color and shadow that provide depth and intensity to the divinely crafted mosaic of your life.

However, at this moment you are probably too close to the picture to get the sense of this. Neither are you feeling particularly prone to philosophize over what is happening. What you want is a meaningful job. But it is important that you understand what is going on in the world, and the ways God has equipped you to cope with it, because this helps to put today's hardships into clearer perspective.

One reason why the workplace is altering so much is that in our generation we are moving away from a "factory" approach to employment that has dominated Western society for the last two hundred years. Whether you have been working on a production line or in a huge bureaucracy, the whole approach to doing almost everything has been modeled on mass production. Processing documents or manufacturing widgets, you have been little more than a small cog in a large machine.

In the end, this pattern of labor has detracted from our humanity. We have been conditioned to function more like clones of Charlie Chaplin when he played the production line worker in his wonderful old silent movie *Modern Times*. Most of us have gotten used to being a mere number, a shuffler of papers, or as its operator, the living extension of a machine, and we have been prepared to do it because it has provided security and a regular paycheck.

The Information Revolution is changing all this. Less and less will intelligent workers be treated as cogs within the wheels of industry. The trend is for employees to become increasingly creative contributors to the end product or service that the organization or network is marketing. In the long term, our God-given creativity and ability to make decisions is going to be an important part of our work.

It is possible that tomorrow's workplace will be a better and more fulfilling place than today's, but this is going to take time to coalesce. Meanwhile, all of us are discovering that there is a dark side of this process in our society, as we attempt a paradigm shift from an old to a seemingly endless procession of new ways of doing things, and unemployment is part of that dark side.

It has been extremely difficult for the average worker to think of himself or herself as a professional with a vocation if the job entailed, say, processing documents exactly as 350 other people process them. And if you spend year after year on a production line without being asked to make any creative contribution to the way the car or the refrigerator is built, then it must seem at times that work has robbed you of everything that makes you a unique human being in the eyes of your fellows and of God.

If you have a vocation, you are called to be God's representative in the place God has put you, be it for one week or ten years. You are asked to make a creative contribution to the well-being of the organization, which you hope and pray will improve the lot of other human beings, the nation, and the world. Then it might well become necessary for you to move on and do something else. A period between positions is a time of preparation for the next chapter of your odyssey, the next part of the call to serve God in a particular setting.

Avoid Nostalgia

I can detect a little voice at the back of your head saying, "I'm not sure I want a vocation that might promise more periods like the one I am going through at the moment." Maybe you yearn for a more traditional career like your parents had. From this perspective in time that probably seems free of the painful consequences of living in a world passing through such transition and uncertainty. I hear you—but I urge you to put such thoughts as far from your mind as you can. This revolution won't throw itself into reverse, and when you are back in work, you may discover there are many benefits about living in such times that you may not be able to see at the moment.

Only a small minority will find positions that promise lifetime employment in the future. As we have seen already, the days of even these stable kinds of careers seem numbered. Try to overcome nostalgia. The secret of moving ahead as a person and as a servant of God is to do your best to embrace the positive facets of these new realities, and to allow them to shape your life accordingly.

Perhaps there are aspects of this emerging world of work that may be unacceptable to you, but you cannot walk away from it in its entirety. Only by being part of this new wave will you be an agent of transformation, able to help with the construction of a better future for both yourself and your children. Management guru Tom Peters has suggested that this period of transition is likely to last for another twenty to thirty years, so you're going to have to wrestle with its consequences for a very long time.

What's happened is that you've been bounced out of a rut. It is uncomfortable to be without those familiar points of reference that previously provided the backdrop against which you lived your life. But handled properly, this mysterious future will be laden with endless fascinating opportunities for your personal and spiritual growth. Ruts do not facilitate growth, but crises do. You can complain all you want about the agony of unemployment, but if that is all you do, you are unlikely to reach the level of personal and spiritual maturity of which you are capable, and you are going to make it more difficult to find yourself a new job.

Andrew is a longtime friend of mine who lives in the Southwest. His whole life and career literally dissolved around him some years ago. In his early forties, he was forced to make a totally new beginning. I will not pretend these last years have been easy for him as he has attempted to retool himself for a new future. But he has managed to make a good new beginning in a fresh direction, as well as fulfill his duties as parent and spouse.

His one-man accounting and financial planning business is flourishing, and there are new and exciting goals toward which he is now striving. To me, Andrew has become a symbol that it can be done—it is possible for a person to pick up the gauntlet thrown down by this fast-paced world and with God's help to start over.

So I urge you to embrace change; don't run from it. Initially, it might be a little like hugging a grizzly bear, but once you get beyond the discomfort you will discover new horizons to be reached and new challenges that blow aside the cobwebs that so easily gather in the nooks and crannies of our lives. Today's workers are like settlers staking out the claims on the prairies of a brand-new world.

CHAPTER FIVE

CHURCHES, CLERGY, AND YOUR JOB HUNT

"Where does my help come from?" asked the psalmist. And he answered, "My help comes from the Lord."
Yes, Lord, and my help comes from you too. Therefore I look to you for your help
in my daily life and work,
in times of need, illness, and anxiety,
in facing my problems and difficulties.
So, come what may, I meet each day with serene faith and quietness of heart, the Lord being my helper.

Frank Colquhoun

The first piece of advice I always give to job hunters is "Get help." The second is "Begin by looking for it at the church." Advice like this often surprises people.

"I didn't know churches were able to help me" is a response echoed again and again by plenty of out-of-work Christians all over the country. Some folks who say this are people who might have been deeply involved in their congregation for years. Once they discover that a Christian community can be of assistance, a whole new dimension is added to the search for meaningful employment.

It is always a great temptation to keep the bad news of being out of work to yourself, perhaps because you feel humiliated by it and are ashamed of yourself. This temptation needs to be fought and overcome. Only by sharing your situation will you find the help you need, and the caring Christian community is always a good starting place.

Those on the fringes or uninvolved in church life are even more surprised, exclaiming, "What, the church can help *me* with my search—how?" If you are part of this group, then you will know that many folk think the church is the place of last resort if they are in trouble, rather than a supporting community in a time of need like this. Perhaps you perceive Christians as too heavenly minded to be of any earthly good, or that the churches are only interested in running soup kitchens for those who are *really* down on their luck, or Bible studies for the "religious."

I'm biased, I know, but I can't think of a better place to get encouragement when it comes to making a fresh start. Not only does the Christian community have an innate capacity to gather around and tend the wounds of those who are in distress, but church people can be a terrific source of leads, and these are vital to an effective network. Without a strong network you considerably reduce your chances of getting back into meaningful employment. Even if the church only provides pastoral support and T.L.C., it is making an enormous contribution to your efforts. But many churches have gone way beyond this; they have helped establish support groups specifically designed for those who are plying their skills in the job market.

Job Hunt Support Groups

In parish halls and church basements all around the country, groups of men and women without regular employment gather once or twice a week to give one another mutual support and encouragement. Many who find themselves drawn into these gatherings may not have ventured further than the church parking lot in years. Some of them are, perhaps, a little fearful about plunging into this setting. But when they discover these groups are a nonthreatening environment where they can find help to shape up their résumé and develop tools that will enable them to put their lives back together again, misgivings often turn into enthusiasm.

A few years ago, a friend of mine was pastor of a lively Episcopal parish in Charlotte, North Carolina. Knowing of my interest in career searches, he began talking to me about the job hunt group that had coalesced around some people who were out of work in his congregation. At that time, the banking industry was in deep trouble. As a major banking center, Charlotte was being particularly hard hit when some of the local banks that had large departments there started merging, streamlining their operations, or downsizing. Literally thousands who thought they were secure for life were laid off as the financial service industry set about transforming itself.

Many gifted people who found themselves without work had never before been forced to go out looking for new employment. Gradually, the handful who had used one of the Sunday school classrooms became several hundred job seekers who gathered once or twice a week in the parish hall. Not only were they able to support each other through the trauma, but also they set about arranging seminars and shared contacts with their fellow job hunters. A camaraderie developed that was reminiscent of front-line troops.

Only a minority of these job hunters had been members of that particular congregation when they lost their jobs. Some belonged to other churches, while some had no religious affiliation at all. A few who were spiritually unconnected wound up becoming part of the parish as a result of the group, even though there was never any pressure put on people to sign up. They were simply accepted into the job search group as they were, and no inappropriate personal questions were asked. The primary task of the group was to offer a forum to those who were unemployed and to their families as they traveled across that barren desert of joblessness back into the work force. But as we will see in a later chapter, times of crisis like this are occasions when many people find themselves asking fundamental questions about the meaning of life. It is hardly surprising that for some this painful change eventually leads to a deep and genuine Christian commitment.

A job hunt by its very nature is a one-man, one-woman task. It can be very lonely. When you are looking for a job you sense you are very much on your own and out in the cold. What makes things even worse is that the great majority of your friends are not only gainfully employed, but they may not even appear to be that interested in your plight. This is not unnatural, because in your situation some of them see their own deepest fears about unemployment being lived out.

> *Times of crisis are occasions when many people find themselves asking fundamental questions about the meaning of life.*

You would be unnatural if you didn't feel alone and isolated. Even with the wholehearted backing of family and loved ones, it is inevitable for you to feel separated from the mainstream of daily life. This is why it is so important to seek people who will prop you up and aid you through this uncomfortable time. This is why it is vital that you belong to a group who are in the same boat as yourself. Such an environment is able to provide wonderful encouragement when you feel as if you are close to your wits' end. There is little point multiplying your stress by trying to play the "Lone Ranger." A support group can save you from going around looking as if you have just experienced a month of wet Sundays, when it is absolutely vital that you look upbeat—even if you don't feel it.

If you can't find a group in your area, why not approach a friendly pastor and ask whether the parish would be willing to host such a gathering. If the pastor says yes, put an ad in the local paper. Unless you live in a tiny rural community, I can guarantee you'll be in business.

I was reading a church newspaper I don't normally see just recently, and stumbled across a fascinating article about one such group in Richmond, Virginia. It was the brainchild of a professional in his fifties whose career had once been his whole life. He had lived for his job twenty-four hours a day for as long as he could remember. In a takeover scramble, his position was eliminated, and he really thought his useful life had come to an end. He slipped into a deep depression as the "Thanks, but no thanks" letters started piling up on his desk at home. But the group proved to be his salvation. After months as the anchorperson of the gathering meeting in their church, his self-esteem had been restored, even if it was taking him longer to find gainful employment than he had expected.

The Help Clergy Can Offer

I spent a considerable chunk of my early years in the work force pastoring parishes on both sides of the Atlantic. Despite this, I never cease to be surprised by the huge cross section of people clergy get to know in the cities, towns, and suburbs where they work. Pastors are able to cross social and professional barriers far more easily than almost any other group. This makes clergy natural enablers in a job search. Many clergy are encouragers by nature. Add to that their mental "database" of contacts, and you have someone who can make a real difference to your job search.

I want to dispel the misconception that pastors are functionaries whose interests seldom reach beyond the traditional rites of passage (births, deaths, marriages), weekly worship services, and the well-being of the souls of their immediate congregation. The scope of most clergy jobs is far wider than this. Because of the people they know, the majority have ready-made networks whose tentacles can reach with extraordinary rapidity into some of the most helpful places for someone looking for work.

Supporting people who need work is one of those life transitions for which many clergy are incredibly well-equipped. Most pastors are happy to assist not just church members but people whose contact with their parish might be peripheral. Unhappily, not many job searchers draw their clergy into the hunt, and very few grasp the ways that they can help them. This is disappointing because both sides would be the beneficiaries.

Our God is concerned about the whole person—not just the soul. He gives each of us a unique set of gifts not only to serve him, but to provide immense fulfillment in our daily work as well. If it is the job of the clergy to help people develop their spiritual gifts, why shouldn't they be deeply involved in the business of assisting you as you attempt to put your whole package of talents to use in your career?

One caveat: If you approach your pastor for job hunting advice, remember that he or she is not a professional career counselor. Seminary training tends to help a pastor develop listening and counseling skills, and some ministers or priests might even be able to critique your résumé. But most are better equipped to be brought into the process once they have the final copy of your curriculum vitae in front of them, and they know something about you and your background. With information in hand, pastors can help you review your situation and be sounding boards as you attempt to point yourself in the right direction.

I know few clergy who will not have useful suggestions about employment opportunities as you go through your situation with them. Obviously, if you are a "regular" at church, the pastor is going to know a lot more about your strengths and weaknesses, and will be able to be more specific with advice.

Today's clergy don't live their lives in religious ivory towers! An increasing number have had extensive experience in other fields prior to ordination, so they can probably discuss career problems and opportunities with reference to a diverse professional past of their own. I know clergy who were everything from computer analysts to college professors prior to ordination, and one of my ministerial friends ran a very successful construction company. The former pastor of the little parish to which I belong drove a tractor-trailer for many years, while one priest I know is also one of the finest eye doctors!

"Second-career" ministers know from personal experience how hard it is to change employment horses—they are likely to understand exactly what you are going through. For many of them, the transition into ordained ministry may have been costly, both financially and emotionally. This means they can give you down-to-earth suggestions about how to handle these unsettling months, as well as spiritual and emotional advice about how to cope.

The Pastor's Network

Let's go back to the pastor's network. As I have said, it is probably one of the biggest assets the pastor has to offer. Clergy are natural networkers, their congregations serving as ready-made starting points. If your pastor has been in the locality for a long time, he or she will be familiar with the community and the people in town who make things happen. A few phone calls or referrals, and you may find yourself linked with people who can make a tremendous difference as you pursue your career objectives.

If your pastor is new in town, her or his assistance will obviously be more limited, but don't write it off. Clergy have colleagues both in their own church and in a variety of other denominations who have the contacts they lack. Most clergy belong to ecumenical or interfaith ministerial associations that can act as a referral network for your pastor if he or she arrived in town quite recently. Or better still, get your pastor to introduce you to others he or she might know.

When I moved from Massachusetts to an Episcopal church in Rochester, New York, in the late seventies, I knew no one. During my first few months there I had little idea who the funeral directors were, let alone who would be a good person to help someone else find new work. More often than not, it was my Presbyterian neighbor who came to the rescue when I needed that kind of advice. He had worked in that part of the world for more than twenty years, and he knew Upstate New York like the back of his hand. I would have gotten into deep trouble without him!

"But I Don't Know the Pastor!"

Even as I write these words I can hear a thousand objections forming in your mind about sharing career concerns with a member of the clergy. These objections scream loudly and persistently, especially if you had a bad experience in the past, or you find pastors and priests a little forbidding. So here are some responses to a few of the questions you might be asking:

Question: "If I share private information, will it be spread all over town?"
Answer: Not if the pastor is any good at the job. Clergy are trained to be confidential and can even get into legal trouble if they don't keep things to themselves. Many are used to hearing all sorts of secrets and confessions from members of their congregations. They would lose their credibility if they didn't maintain those confidences. Most can be trusted to keep their months shut on those things you don't want gabbed around.

Question: "Will it cost me anything?"
Answer: In almost all cases, of course not. Meeting with people in need is one of the many facets of a pastor's life. Those who have particular expertise or counseling qualifications might

make a charge, but they will warn you beforehand so you will know what you're getting yourself into. However, if a member of the clergy has gone to a great deal of trouble on your behalf, you may wish to acknowledge the ministry in some way. In this case, many clergy would appreciate a small donation to their discretionary fund once you are back in full employment. These funds would then be used to help the range of people who visit a pastor looking for help.

Question: "How many times can I visit a member of the clergy for help with my job search?"
Answer: That varies. Although Sunday is the big day for most clergy, they have more than enough to keep them busy during the week. The majority of pastors I know have time-consuming jobs, which they do conscientiously, often working very long hours. They do not appreciate it if their services are abused. When I was a parish priest, I found that if a person kept returning even when I was unable to help him or her, I would refer that individual to another professional with the skill to make a difference. Counselors and therapists normally charge a fee.

Question: "Is the pastor going to try to convert me? I'm not much of a churchgoer."
Answer: In some Christian traditions this is possible, but you will be aware of this before linking up with that particular pastor and church. In my experience, most clergy are no more comfortable with the idea of ramming the gospel down your throat than you are. Most will respect your request if you ask them not to offer unwanted spiritual advice. Of course, pastors are likely to see your situation from a religious perspective—and as we will see in the next chapter, foxhole religion does have a nasty habit of turning into the real thing!

If you are looking for a new job, then you should make use of all the contacts you can find. As well as being in touch with the Chamber of Commerce, professional associations, and the like, members of the clergy ought to be on your list of people who need to be consulted. If you don't know how to make the initial contact, just identify the church you want to be in touch with, call the church office, and make an appointment through the secretary. Remember, nothing ventured, nothing gained.

Help with Other Problems

Many of those looking for new positions are struggling with all sorts of other problems. One survey of 15,000 job seekers uncovered the frightening statistic that 75 percent of them were either facing or in the midst of or recovering from a breakdown of their marriage. Even if this is not true for you, I almost always find that hard times like these put inordinate amounts of pressure on your dearest relationships.

Like almost all married couples, my wife and I have had our ups and downs. When I was under career stress, our marriage teetered on the edge for quite a while. It was the clergy who supported us with great love and care through those difficult times. Even if you came to the church only looking for help finding a new position, you may find that the Christian community is able to carry you through some difficult domestic episodes.

One man I talked to recently was at his wits' end with his spouse. While he was stretched to the limits trying to find a new job, and worried sick about making ends meet, all she would do was whine that he wasn't working hard enough to land a new position—even though he was going at it full force. This was her way of expressing the anxiety she felt about their plight. Fortunately, a pastor was there to help them through this awkward episode, and I am delighted to say my friend is now back at work again.

Some larger churches are in a position to give financial counseling, even to lend money from a revolving fund to those struggling to keep themselves afloat. Making ends meet can become increasingly difficult if a job search is protracted. In my last parish, which was not an especially big one, we had several people who were skilled at building and managing budgets. If members of the congregation got themselves into financial trouble, they would help the family develop a budget that would enable them to live within their means. Once that budget was in place, they would monitor the situation until stability returned.

Sometimes out of this ministry came the information that So-and-So was not going to make it financially. Such information was handled in the strictest confidence, but it enabled several of us to put together funds and even food to help them over the hump. I must warn you that it doesn't happen like this in every congregation; but I have seen literally thousands of dollars given away like this with little hope that it would ever be paid back.

Every job hunter needs moral and spiritual support because there are times when you are likely to feel terribly alone. I don't know of a better place to get it than within the bosom of the Christian community. God's people don't want to see lives ruined, families destroyed, and individuals humiliated. I can guarantee that almost every church in this land will do its very best to help the job hunter over the hump and to that promised new beginning.

C H A P T E R
SIX

THERE'S NOTHING WRONG WITH FOXHOLE RELIGION

Times without number in the story of men's search for reality,
beginning with the historic fact of Jesus Christ, the "grace" of
His Person and work, men have been led on to dare to believe
in the love of God and in that fellowship of the Holy Spirit which
finds its chief expression in the Church of God. God moves men,
and brings them to Himself, in an infinite variety of ways. There
is no set order or stereotyped pattern. But very often it proves to
be the case that Christ's grace is the doorway, the entrance-gate,
to a man's realisation of God's love and the Spirit's fellowship.
Donald Coggan, *Prayers of the New Testament*

There Aren't Many Atheists on a Battlefield

On June 6, 1944, hundreds of naval vessels of all shapes and sizes made a choppy crossing of the English Channel. Rolling waves, blowing winds, and paralyzing fear caused thousands of the soldiers packed into the landing craft to become ill. Each passing minute brought them a little closer to France, where they would be expected to face the worst the Nazis had to hurl at them.

I'm told there weren't many atheists or agnostics that day. Whether British, American, French, Canadian, Australian, Polish, or even Gurkha, few of those frightened men did not turn their anxieties into prayer during those final hours before the

D-Day landings took place on the beaches of Normandy in northern France.

Forty-five years later, another army sat in the Saudi Arabian desert preparing to liberate Kuwait. The men and women of Desert Storm began showing an unexpected interest in God as the instant for live warfare approached. When the conflict was about to come to a head, I found myself listening to a chaplain just returned from the Gulf describe packed Sunday services, a run on Bibles, and an uncharacteristic concern among the GIs and troops of other nationalities for the well-being of their souls.

Many sneer at "foxhole religion," but I am not among them. It is the most natural thing in the world to turn our mind toward our Creator when we sense our backs are up against the wall, and we wonder whether we will get out of a situation alive.

The Meaning of the Gospel When You're in a "Foxhole"

Those who despise foxhole religion have misunderstood the gospel and the real task of Christian fellowship. The church is not a shrine to which those who consider themselves perfect come to pat themselves on their collective backs, although I have to admit an awful lot of that happens. Rather, it is a hospital for the frightened, broken, and sinful. In every congregation of every denomination, there are people whose initial motives for being part of a worshiping community are less than pure. Perhaps they arrived in that congregation because they were wounded or hurting or fearful—or maybe just chasing a prospective date whom they knew would be there each week!

A well-known show-business personality belonged to the congregation I pastored in London nearly twenty-five years ago. His presence attracted the star-struck, so a steady stream of his fans passed through our Sunday services. A majority left, some of them deeply disillusioned when they discovered their idol was not that much different from anyone else. But interestingly, others stayed and became part of our church community.

Some who came to gaze with ardor on their favorite singer now serve Christ in various places all over the world. One woman who had both nursing and managerial skills later ran a major medical relief operation in Africa. These young people's initial motives for coming to church were questionable to say the least, but in the end their original reasons for coming were superseded by God.

> *It is the most natural thing in the world to turn our mind toward our Creator when we sense our backs are up against the wall, and we wonder whether we will get out of a situation alive.*

There is nothing wrong with giving religion a try—especially when you are struggling to find your way across the battlefield of unemployment. Your motive for being in church ought not to be the issue at this point. If you are frightened and scared, there is no better place than the Christian community to find friends who will help you through your troubles—and a God who understands your plight.

When there have been massive lay offs and restructurings—which usually mean a loss of jobs—often churches have been at the forefront of the human recovery effort. As we have seen already, some have formed self-help groups to enable workers to get back into the job market—and at any one time there are thousands of such groups in the United States. For many persons, groups like this have been a lifeline during this very difficult personal transition.

The church is a good place to explore starting over. As we have seen, it is important for job searchers to include parishes in their networks. Pastors and priests are generally helpful people, and they can provide both contacts and counseling that won't cost you an arm and a leg. But if your reason for looking in the direction of the church is merely utilitarian, then I suggest you dig a little deeper.

Foxhole Religion Often Turns into the Real Thing

I need to warn you that what may start off as foxhole religion often has the strange habit of mutating into the real thing. Some of those who survived the Nazi pounding on the beaches of northern France on that June day long ago were never the same again. A now-retired English bishop, who was a young chaplain in the British Army in 1944, used to regale us when we were seminarians with stories of God at work transforming the lives of soldiers in northern France during that historic battle for Europe. Some of those soldiers who surrendered the outcome to the Almighty became lifelong servants of Christ. By the time I made my fumbling start in the ordained ministry in the late 1960s, some of those veterans were the leaders of the church. Such stories can be repeated time and again in the history of the Christian faith. God has the habit of meeting us at the most unlikely times and places!

But let me return to the parish in London for a moment. The fans and kids might have come to gaze mindlessly at a guy who came on stage, strummed a guitar, and sang songs. In the end it was not the entertainer who captivated some of them, but the message they heard from the pulpit, which they watched acted out around the altar, or that they experienced in the lives of other young people who packed the pews.

> *"God has the habit of meeting us at the most unlikely times and places!"*

Job hunters may initially come because of the support and encouragement the church provides. There's nowhere else to go, and they are desperate. But as they wrestle with unemployment, other issues are brought to the surface of their lives. To their amazement, many of them discover God to be gracious and loving—and to their surprise, they find out that *God really is interested in them.* Before they know it, they're in church on Sundays, then at Bible study during the week, then, perhaps, out doing voluntary acts of love for those in more need than themselves. The words that once seemed so passé are now filled with meaning and hope, providing them strength to carry on in the midst of great personal discomfort.

A few years ago, I was presenting the work of the Christian agency which I serve at a church convention. Very early one morning, after having gotten to bed late the night before, I was standing by our exhibit drinking a cup of strong coffee and trying to wake myself up. Suddenly, a tall, middle-aged man was standing in front of me introducing himself. His name was Ned, and he wanted to thank me for several of the articles I had written for the *National Business Employment Weekly.* He had found what I wrote so helpful that on one occasion when he was feeling particularly low he called me—did I remember him? I cannot say I did, but that did not kill the conversation. By now I was wide awake!

He then went on to tell me he had been little more than a social churchgoer until he lost his job following the great Wall Street Crash of October 1987. Unemployment was difficult for him because he was considered too old or overqualified for most of the positions for which he applied. Feeling hurt and dejected, Ned found himself turning to the church for sustenance and help, and in the process had a genuine and life-changing encounter with Jesus Christ. When I met Ned, he was back at work, having moved with his family to a very different part of the country, and now served God as a dedicated lay leader of the little Episcopal church in the town to which his new employment had finally brought them.

We had a wonderful conversation. The process of finding a faith had been the buried treasure, and he had discovered it as a result of his unemployment. Now it was adding a richness to his life he had not imagined possible before. As I said earlier, foxhole religion has this extraordinary tendency under certain circumstances to mutate into the real thing.

While that little church on the corner might look a bit shabby and appear to be fairly insignificant, it is one of the places where you might find help at difficult points in your life. The words sung and spoken there have a power all their own. They possess the ability to delve their way deep into your psyche, because behind them is the power of God. They have the capacity to change and heal you, perhaps making you a better, more complete person than before.

If you are prepared to pay the price Christian discipleship demands, then I would encourage you to pursue it, for there is a God-shaped gap deep in the heart of each one of us.

The Christian gospel is about starting over, and what better moment than these doldrums of your life to make a new beginning? The price is high, because Christ wants *all* of you. But he has already given all of himself for you.

Work Out the Details Later

You might be a little leery about making such a radical move, especially if you and God have not been on speaking terms for a few years. But what you need now is help, and turning in God's direction at a time like this is not a sign of weakness but an acknowledgment of this fact.

In most cases no one is going to try to shove religion down your throat, but will respect your personhood and integrity. It doesn't need to come together all at once either. For most people, particularly those who are in mid-life, it usually evolves over quite a long period. Right now just explore the ways faith in Jesus Christ might make an impact on your life, and work out the details of your church relationship in the future when things are more settled.

I've seen people who can work wonders with a financial statement, yet couldn't find the first chapter of the book of Genesis—let alone the rest of the Bible—even if they were offered a million dollars! At least one such searcher I can think of ended up as a Sunday school teacher and a leading member of the church board.

At the beginning, there is no need to get hung up on the niceties of religion. You need help, and the Christian community is eager to give it. And even if you discover this is not for you, the church is happy to nurture you through these hard times, not because it expects some kind of reward but because you are part of God's creation, made in his image. One great Christian said that the church is the only organization in the world that exists for the benefit of those outside it. Many of us believe that with all our hearts.

But don't forget—there is power in those religious niceties, a power that has subtlety and strength way beyond the understanding of the most incisive human mind. Even though I have lived with the gospel of Jesus Christ for the whole of my adult life, it still has the ability to surprise me, taking my breath away with its audacity.

What Happens to Those Who Find Fellowship with God as a Result of a Career Crisis?

In most cases, these people seem to find their way back into a job that is not too dissimilar to the one they left. Their skills and talents are put to use in the economy in ways that they know and understand from past experience. People like Tony, the unemployed oil executive we met at the beginning of this book who is now an Episcopal priest, or the woman who runs medical relief work in Africa are exceptions. Some, because of God's guidance during this time of deepening Christian commitment, do find their way toward a full-time religious vocation. I assure you, they are a tiny minority, and seldom do such calls happen immediately after a life-changing spiritual encounter. Right now

I am corresponding with a computer programmer whose faith was enriched and reinforced during a time out of work and whom I got to know during that bleak period of his life. He's now thinking about offering himself for ordination. I don't know whether he will get there—we will see.

More likely, you will find yourself getting more deeply involved in Christian activities as your faith grows and matures. You may find that you have skills that can be used by the church as it cares for those in need, attempts to manage its budget, or educates its children in the Christian way. I would hazard a guess that wherever you find yourself fitting in, you will gain great pleasure and satisfaction from these opportunities and challenges, and you will grow as a person as well.

Those who come to a new kind of faith through the experience of unemployment are also likely to find that the church is a new source of lasting friendships. Just recently, I had dinner with some folks in Texas. I'd never met any of them before, but we had a wonderful evening getting to know each other. Each of them was able to confirm that meeting new friends had been an overwhelmingly positive experience of the Christian church during a time of great upheaval in their lives.

A Christian commitment is not a sign of weakness. Rather, it is evidence that people have gotten to know themselves well enough to realize that without a spiritual component, their lives are not well-rounded. It does not matter whether a man or woman discovers this when young, when everything is going well, or when in a foxhole with the shells raining down on his or her head. The important thing is to discover that through Jesus Christ people are able to fill that God-shaped gap in their hearts, and that he has a will and purpose for their lives.

Right now there is no need to worry about details; they will work themselves out later. This moment is the time to take advantage of all the church, and the people who belong to it, can offer you. You might eventually discover that being a part of the Christian family is not for you. That's okay.

Faith's object

Lord, we do not ask for great faith but for faith in a great Saviour.

We have come to see that the efficacy of our faith depends not on its size but on its object. And we know full well the true object of our faith.

Therefore we pray that we may run the race before us with our eyes fixed on *Jesus,* on whom faith depends from start to finish: Jesus, who endured the shameful cross and is now seated at the right hand of the throne of God.

(Based on Hebrews 12. 1-2)

THE JOURNAL OF YOUR JOB HUNT

*The lowtide is the winter of our lives; it is a time of bareness and
death. Yet it is also a time of strange beauty, a time of purity—and
purifying. In winter we see things that we have never seen before.*
David Adam, *Tides & Seasons*

At the back of the bottom righthand drawer of my office desk
are a dozen or more hardbound notebooks. Anyone stumbling
across them and starting to read would mistake their contents for
the random jottings of a disjointed and occasionally demented
mind! Actually, they are my journals—the almost daily
autobiographic record of my life's ups and downs for much of
the last twenty-five years.

My journals are intensely personal. Only in the unlikely event
that I become rich, famous, or both would anyone other than me
be interested in reading the steady accumulation of words
recorded with the passage of time. I am not always a disciplined
page-a-day journal writer, but most weeks anything from one to
five entries are made. I tend to scribble in these books more often
when things are going badly than when I am on a high. In good
times the diary sometimes remains untouched for days. When I
went on a recent business trip and found I had left my journal at

home, I felt as if a vital part of my spiritual anatomy had been temporarily lost.

Rummaging through my desk some months ago, looking for something that had gotten lost in the jungle of paper, pens, and rubber bands, I ran across my journals. Feeling nostalgic, I found myself dipping into what I had written when my career was at a frightening crossroad. For almost an hour, I was diverted from pressing work, as I followed my anguished progress through the words that had spilled onto those always receptive pages.

I have friends whose careers seem to be a steady, gentle ascent from one job to another, with apparent effortless ease. For me, almost every job transition in more than a quarter of a century has been a crisis! The comments I shared with my journal during those tumultuous times are illuminating. Not only did I say a few perceptive (as well as some rude) things about the process through which I was passing, but I wrote down much that spoke volumes about myself. During those intense periods of "reality therapy," which is what a job search often is, I was forced to do a lot of growing, and my journal reflects it.

Journaling and a New Job

By now you have read four paragraphs all about me, and have yet to discover what this has to do with looking after yourself while searching for a new job. Have patience, and I will show you all—as my old Irish philosophy professor used to say when puzzlement crept across the brows of his students!

If your only concern at this pivotal moment in your life is staying sane and finding a new source of income, then I suggest you cut your losses here and go on to the next chapter. Important as a new position is, if you are eager to make something more out of this career transition by turning it into an exciting period of personal growth, then keep reading. Journaling can be a wonderful teacher when we are in the midst of adversity.

The life that is not reflected upon tends to become bland and shallow, often unsatisfactory to the one who lives it, and almost always a disappointment to those encountering it either in leisure activities or in the workplace. A journal helps you to meditate upon yourself and the events that are shaping your present and future. This is a good reason to make a journal an important adjunct to a job search. I encourage you to bear in mind that this interlude is often one of the most formative anyone ever experiences.

The expert comment I like best about journaling comes from Morton Kelsey, who said in his book *Adventure Inward*: "By recording who and what we are, our feelings, our hopes and goals, we break the hard crust of our selves and allow the depth of us to bubble into sight."[1] Harvey Mackay, whose books *Swim with the Sharks Without Being Eaten Alive* and *Beware of the Naked Man Who Offers You His Shirt,* which have topped *The New York Times* best-seller lists, echoes Father Kelsey. In his job search book, *Sharkproof,* Mackay writes about this episode: "Take time to turn inward, to review your thoughts and experiences, to give your mind a chance to work."[2]

While it is impossible to totally remake ourselves, keeping a journal is a discipline that forces us to dig deeply into who we are. When we do so, we are better able to grasp not only the secrets of our hidden self, but also all the external factors that are shaping us. My journal is almost as good as a therapist or even a "father confessor." Indeed, certain psychotherapists encourage their clients to keep a journal not only of their waking life but also of their dreams.

Some things I have written in that collection of books I have never shared with another soul—not even my wife. I would go so far as to say my journal is probably the easiest place in the world for me to be totally honest about myself with God. This is not always so with diarists. Count Leo Tolstoy, whose books *War and Peace* and *Anna Karenina* are among the greatest

1. Morton Kelsey, *Adventure Inward* (Minneapolis: Augsburg, 1980), p. 21.
2. Harvey Mackay, *Sharkproof* (New York: Harper Business, 1993), p. 55.

novels ever written, found it impossible to separate fact from his fictitious imaginings. Tolstoy deliberately wrote his journals for a wider audience than just himself and God. He shared his journals with his wife, using them to tell her either how much he loved her or, as they got older and their relationship soured into bitter hatred, how much he despised her. Perhaps as he became more famous, the novelist perceived that one day his diaries would be published. At any rate, Tolstoy's very self-conscious productions are a reminder that the best kind of journal is personal and private—something between you and your Creator—only then will you be truly honest.

> *"By recording who and what we are, our feelings, our hopes and goals, we break the hard crust of ourselves and allow the depth of us to bubble into sight."*
>
> *–Morton Kelsey*
> *Adventure Inward*

I started my journal at about the time I began looking for my first professional position. Despite having recently gotten married, I felt vulnerable as I put my life on the line for the first time and went hunting for that all-important job. Writing about the experience began out of the basic instinct of wanting to understand what was happening. There is no better time to commence journaling than at this crucial period of a job search, when you are putting yourself under the scrutiny of potential employers as well as looking for a new tomorrow.

The whole idea of a journal might be very frightening to you. Perhaps you are not used to writing about yourself and your feelings. Maybe you find it difficult to string words together on a page. Whatever your resistance might be, consider trying journaling for a few weeks to see whether you can get into the habit of journaling. Scattered through the remainder of this chapter are suggestions you might find helpful and may give you an idea of how to get started with a journal of your own.

A Life History

First, go out and buy a notebook you like. It doesn't have to be very expensive, but a book that is attractive is always much easier to write in than one whose appearance does not appeal to you. Then set aside a couple of days to write down the salient features of your life from your earliest recollections until now.

To put a lot of hours into an exercise like this may seem a waste of time when you think you should be getting your résumé together or contacting people who can help you find a job. However, I promise you will discover that this time spent looking backward can pay huge dividends in the long run. You are on a journey. How do you know where you should be going if you don't have much of an idea from where you have come?

What I'm asking is that you put your activist agenda on hold for a few hours and look inward—it is excellent preparation for the hard footwork of the job search that lies ahead. This is a way of getting a better fix on who you are, rather than all the jobs you have done in the past. I guarantee that as you write your autobiography, long-forgotten things about yourself will emerge. Some of these submerged gems may hold valuable clues for the way ahead and serve as helpful reminders of past failures and successes. Half-lost memories and unfulfilled hopes are bound to emerge from your subconscious. It still may not be too late to turn those forgotten dreams into vibrant realities. But even if it is, knowing what's there will at least put you in the position to administer "decent Christian burial" to longings that, like old banana peels strewn in your path, could cause a nasty accident.

In addition, reviewing your life and career will help you to identify salient factors you might otherwise have overlooked, skills or experiences that are crucial to your *curriculum vitae,* or ideas that could make a difference in an interview. When your life story has been spilled out onto paper, you may want to rework your résumé because this exercise has uncovered so much information you might have forgotten.

Résumés should reflect your real self, and this exercise will help yours do just that. Even if you do not feel it necessary to modify your résumé in the light of this process, I am certain you will be able to identify some of the motivation behind many of your past moves, and the development of present skills and interests.

When you have your story in place you will be ready for your journal. In effect, throughout your job search you will be adding to the tale of your life on a daily basis. You may find that having done this during your search process, you will want to keep it up for the rest of your life because it is a helpful spiritual exercise. Journal writing is like a daily emotional and psychological housecleaning! I always feel much better after I have made my entry.

Recording your story is excellent preparation for a job search. Everyone I know who has done it—and I have recommended this exercise to most people who have sought my help—has learned vital truths about himself or herself that would otherwise have been lost.

The Journal as Campaign Log

Like a ship on an ocean voyage, a career campaign requires a log. Whom you talked with, what was said, leads you ought to follow up can all be part of your journal. Fail to keep a log, and you are likely to forget pertinent facts, contacts, and possibilities. Like a person wandering around lost in the desert, you will cover the same ground several times, or worse still, miss wonderful opportunities because of the sieve-like quality of your memory—and even the people with the finest memories often find their recall lets them down during the stress of a career transition. For example, you would be amazed how much harm you can do by forgetting a small thing like a thank-you letter to someone who's given assistance and whom you accidentally overlooked. Those thank yous are very, very important. Not only is it courteous to express your gratitude for help given, but it inevitably widens your network and gains you allies as well.

What you write and whom you write to can be recorded in your journal, as well as the way you feel about that relationship. This person might have been the conduit through which a perfect job opportunity could have come. Let me repeat: Most of us tend to be more forgetful when we are under pressure and, as you have probably found out already, a job search is *the* most stressful occupation.

First and foremost, your journal is your daily log. Something to be completed at the end of each day's hunting, it is a vital adjunct to your Rolodex, Filofax, or the Sidekick program on your computer, which records your schedule. Every well-organized person should keep a daily log, but how many do? You might be able to get away without one when there are others in the office to jog your memory, but job hunters are on their own; aids to memory are crucial. A career campaign is more like a marathon than a 100-yard dash; journaling is one of those techniques to help fend off the loneliness of the long-distance runner.

The Journal as Confidant

A journal is more than a hygienic record of the day's goings-on. It should contain your reflections on those events, your fears, and your expectations. My journal has always been a straight-from-the-gut production. I write down how I feel about myself, the people who cross my path, my joys, and the troubles that are making life a misery at the moment.

Sometimes I use my journal to ventilate, at other times it becomes my confidant as I unwrap conundrums that have confused relationships at home or at work. Journaling helps me to untie those knots in my stomach that tend to take my appetite away. As job hunters go into the marketplace, they come face to face with perplexing aspects of the inner life which should not be left unresolved. The turmoil accompanying a challenge like finding a new job is similar to stirring the mud at the bottom of your psychological pond with a stick. Thinking through these issues using pen and paper can go a long way toward clearing the water.

It is especially important to reflect on questions interviewers ask. Usually they will raise routine, even mundane, concerns. But once in a while a shrewd questioner puts a finger on something of deep personal significance, things about yourself of which you may be only partially aware. By recording these on the pages of your journal, you will not only be sharpening your self-understanding, but also readying yourself for the next interviewer. Perhaps you will use your journal to discuss how you ought to have answered a question you fluffed badly.

After sixteen years as an Episcopal priest, I burned out on parish ministry and went looking for work in a different area. It wasn't until someone said, "Richard, I don't understand why you are considering quitting the church's ministry" that I realized that was not really what I wanted at all. I was having my problems with God, it was true, and these needed unraveling, but all I wanted was to be something other than a parish priest in the life of the church for a little while. Subsequently, I discovered there were facets of ministry for which I was better suited. I spilled a lot of ink thinking this one out, but I eventually got there—with my journal's help!

Many people I talk with today are scared of digging too deeply into their soul. Instead of asking uncomfortable questions, they attempt to drown the inner voice with noise—everything from parties and television to the ubiquitous "Walkman." The result is one-dimensional people overfull with undigested thoughts and ideas about themselves and their work. This means they are spiritually and emotionally stunted, and such immaturity can come out to your detriment in a job interview.

A journal guards against this. If you set aside ten minutes a day to write down your life, you are more likely to come to terms with "the good, the bad, and the ugly" within you. Some may find unpacking the inner self so painful that it is necessary to turn to a counselor or the clergy for help. Asking for assistance is nothing to be afraid of. It is a healthy sign that growth is taking place; your soul is looking for room to stretch now that you are at last giving it some exercise. If you give it some wriggle room, I guarantee you'll be better for it.

Adventuring into the inner depths of your being inevitably unleashes the creativity that is a vital ingredient of a successful job search. Let me use the words of Morton Kelsey again: "A journal properly used is like a playground into which we can step and play when we are alone. It is only a short step from using a journal as a place in which one can play to using one's notebook as the raw material for the creative artistic drive."

Putting Pen to Paper

I'm writing these words on my laptop computer. These days I write little except very personal letters and my journal with a pen. I may be old-fashioned, but it is inconceivable that I would put my journal onto a floppy disk.

The reason for this is twofold. First, it gives me almost primitive satisfaction to start with a clean white page and fill it with words about God, my life, and the state of my soul. Others may not share this feeling and be happier with a computer or tape recorder. Second, it is far too easy to change what you have written when you put it on a computer disk, and I am not into the Orwellian business of revising my own history. The reason I write my articles and books on a computer is that it gives me the opportunity to revise and rewrite. My published work goes through many rewrites before my editors and I are satisfied. But a journal is different. Once you have gotten this particular day of your life into writing, it is captured forever—for better or for worse.

Years from now, you are likely to return to certain pages of your journal and cringe at what you have said, just as I did when I came across those blacker episodes of my life when searching through my desk. Despite this, you will find yourself wondering at the marvelous way God has been at work in your heart when you re-read your journal. You will begin to see how sins, failures, and disappointments were all raw material the Almighty used to make you a better and more mature person.

Perhaps the most wonderful thing about looking back through my journals is the way I can see God's hand guiding and shaping me through a quarter of a century of ups and downs. Setbacks that seemed to make little sense when I was trapped in the midst of them are given new significance when viewed as part of the larger warp and woof of time. I would say that my journal is a record of God's graciousness to me, as well as the story of my life and my career.

Have I convinced you? Give journaling a try. For those willing to persevere with this age-old discipline, I am certain you will never regret the day you made it part of your routine. Not only that, but I am convinced it will make you more effective in your search for a new beginning.

C H A P T E R

EIGHT

A DISCIPLINED LIFE

O Lord, thou knowest how busy I must be this day. If I forget thee, do not thou forget me.

Sir Joseph Astley's prayer before battle in 1642

The Blight of Disorganization!

While I might be able to organize ideas on a page, my personal life is always rather haphazard. I lose everything from car keys to my wallet with such monotonous regularity that it drives my wife up the wall. Just the other day my reading glasses disappeared and have yet to surface! If I have a perennial New Year resolution, it is to be more organized and efficient. Usually this resolve has become "dead letter" by January 3!

I'm not alone. Poor time management is a characteristic shared by a huge proportion of the human race. A segment of the permanently discombobulated in the population is bound, by the law of averages, to be reading this book! This chapter is about the importance of working hard to ensure you are as orderly as possible while you carry out your career search.

Nothing hobbles a job hunt more than lack of discipline. When we were children, someone else imposed order on our lives. In elementary school, our days were strictly regimented. In college, there were classes to attend and deadlines to meet. Almost every company for which most of us might have worked has had its own operating procedures and clear expectations, which have been clearly spelled out to us. In those situations, it was probably relatively easy to be orderly.

When we find ourselves without work, we are suddenly stripped of the disciplines that have provided a framework for our lives. Now it is our own responsibility to give each day shape and structure. Even if the job hunter is a natural self-starter, an iron will is required if hours, days, and even weeks of valuable search time are not frittered away and lost forever.

I make no apologies for including this chapter about discipline, an unpopular idea in today's world. It is vital that you establish a routine and then stick to it. The question is this: What sort of disciplines do you need? How do you impose them on your life?

Getting Up and Looking Good

I was in England a few years ago when an article jumped at me off the page of the London daily newspaper I happened to be reading. It described in vivid detail the necessity of being disciplined when looking for work. The writer was a journalist who some time before had been laid off due to financial stringencies at his publication. Now that he was back at work, he had been given the opportunity of an editorial page column to share some of his experiences with the paper's readers.

The initial shock of losing his job hit him so hard that during the first few weeks he spent much of the day moping in bed. To make matters worse, he washed and shaved only when he felt like it. On more than one occasion he fell into the temptation of overindulging his taste for beer and Scotch in an attempt to drown his sorrows.

Whether he admitted to realizing it or not I don't recall, but what he was going through was grieving over something similar to a death in the family. This volatile mixture of denial, anger, and a loss of confidence led him to bury himself in bed and bottle until he was ready to reach beyond his immediate misery and depression. Then, ever so gradually, it started to dawn on this hapless writer that he wasn't doing anything useful to get back into employment.

As he lay there one afternoon, wallowing in his misery, he resolved that if he did not mend his ways, his situation would go from bad to worse, and he would end up in the gutter. That thought frightened him. So began the personal reformation that put him back on the road to a regular paycheck.

The first amendment in his life-style was to set the alarm at a reasonable hour in the morning, and then to respond to the bell when it went off. Some mornings he didn't quite succeed, but within a couple of weeks he was back into the routine of rising first thing in the morning. He would wash, shave, and dress—not in casual clothes, but in his *business* suit. He found that by dressing smartly he was able to distinguish clearly a work day from the weekend. This became the symbol that he was going off to work—*looking for work*. Politicians, priests, and marketers know that symbols are far more important than most of us realize.

I have discovered that job hunters tend to succumb far too readily to the temptation to dress down—to defer to the T-shirt and jeans subculture. Maybe I'm a little old-fashioned, but I find that if people dress smartly, they are more inclined to think clearly. When you are on a job search, you need all your wits about you. Besides, looking for work *is* your job for the moment. Even if your search is not likely to take you out of your home all day, still endeavor to prepare for work by dressing as you would if you were going into the office or to an important interview.

Time Management

Having got up, dressed, and breakfasted, our journalist friend made sure he was in the makeshift office he set up for himself in a corner of his apartment by 9:00 A.M. If he had still been in a job, his employer would have expected him to have ridden the train into an office in central London by then, so why not set the discipline of working office hours during his search for new work? He found this routine difficult when he started because he had to impose it upon himself, but once he got over initial lethargy and was into the second week of this regimen, it was much easier to concentrate on the job at hand—finding new employment.

During the middle of the day, he made sure he was seen at one of the journalists' haunts around Fleet Street, which was at that time still the hub of London's newspaper business. This was vital networking, although that word had not come into vogue at that time. It was essential that he be seen in places where journalists and those who hire journalists go.

Having drunk a little too much in his miserable period, he now made sure he had his wits about him. A mind blurred by alcohol will not make people feel confident in you. While there were days when he felt strangely isolated, he knew that if he stayed away too long, people would not think about him when they heard of possible openings. It was career suicide to be out of the loop, so he took seriously the old adage "Out of sight, out of mind."

Persistence

He worked the phones, talking with former colleagues and contacts who might be helpful to him. He undertook exploratory interviews, answered advertisements, and did all the other things a thorough job search demands, keeping a record of his progress and regularly going back over his tracks. This pattern of life prevailed for our reporter for several months. Finally, his efforts paid off. After a search that seemed to have led up hill and down dale, he was hired by the prestigious London paper I found myself reading that morning his article was published.

It would appear his search taught him some sobering lessons, which he was now putting into practice in the workplace. He pointed out that the experience had forced him to inject a discipline into his life that had not been there before, and he was a better journalist as a result of it. He also pointed out that he had learned how important persistence is.

I don't know whether he was exaggerating as he told his tale, as most of us do when we recount our own "war stories." But until that point in his life, he had never really needed to exercise the stickability necessary for landing a new position. Until his job loss, things had tended to drop into his lap; so at first he thought a new job would probably appear that way. When it was obvious it would not, he was forced to change his tactics.

The ability to persevere is not a natural gift. Perseverance is something that grows as we nurture it—like patience and good manners. It is invaluable in every sphere of human activity, not least in the world of work. Too many of us give way to the temptation of letting things go when the going gets tough. Discovering how to persevere may be one of the greatest blessings you receive as a result of your job search.

Job Hunting Is Your Job

A disciplined job hunt is time consuming. Like our journalist friend during his first days without a job, job hunters often spend too much time loafing and too little time looking for work. This leads to disappointment when it comes to the really good employment opportunities. Because these persons aren't out there watching the market like hawks, the real plums pass them by. Finding good work demands that you commit an eight-hour day, five or six days a week, to the search. If you don't, you are likely to be forced to settle for second best.

One young man I know thought he was God's gift to the world of work, and he tried to land a position with a handful of phone calls each week, together with an occasional interview. Needless to say, it took him months to find a job, and then it was a minimum-wage position when he was capable of something a lot better.

People say that other people are lucky when they land something wonderful, but many years ago, as I have recounted already, I discovered fortunate people make their own luck. Oh, there are unexpected breaks and happy coincidences, but these very often follow hard on the heels of a large dose of unadulterated hard work—and perhaps persistent prayer.

> *Set identifiable, measurable goals at the beginning of each week, and then examine your performance regularly.*

Job hunt manuals—such as *What Color Is Your Parachute?*[1] —are filled with clues about how to plan and use your working week wisely. They cannot make you do what needs to be done; that is your responsibility, and the will to do it comes from within you. To win this race, you need both determination and discipline. I will guarantee one thing, however: Persevere with your search and you will in due course find too much rather than too little to fill your day!

It is only reasonable to assume that the more time you give to looking, the more contacts you will have made and the better chances there will be of finding a fulfilling employment opportunity. Set yourself identifiable, measurable goals at the beginning of each week, and then examine your performance regularly. I always try to take stock on Sunday evenings, setting some broad targets for the five or six days ahead of me.

---

1. At the end of this book is a section entitled "To Help You in Your Search." *What Color Is Your Parachute?* and other helpful resources are outlined there.

I have noticed that when people undertake a really determined hunt they often end up with more than one job offer. It was no accident that the journalist whose story I have told in this chapter landed a position at one of the more prestigious London newspapers. Once cured of the "couch potato syndrome," he gave more time each day to looking for work than he might have put into salaried employment.

A Spiritual Discipline

As a Christian, I find that discipline and my spiritual life go hand in hand. When I let my personal spirituality slide, my self-discipline usually evaporates with it. If I want to be focused, then I cannot afford to leave the Almighty out. In the midst of one of the most important periods of your life, like finding new work, it is very shortsighted to push God to the periphery of the process. God needs to be a key player on your team.

Besides, God wants to be an active partner in your job search. You are on a journey toward a new beginning when you are looking for a job. Often you will reach a fork in the road and will need a companion to help you decide which path to take. The Lord God will give you such help if you include him in your planning and preparation for the future. Twists and turns of divine logic may seem puzzling, but in retrospect you will be able to look back and see how he has guided and directed your life.

If you commit eight hours a day to a disciplined hunt for opportunities, each day make sure you put time with God into that schedule. Perhaps when you sit down at your desk in the morning, before anything else can divert your attention, open your Bible, read, meditate, or pray over a passage using some simple devotional aid or set of Bible reading notes. If you've never tried anything like this before, ask for help from a pastor or a Christian friend you trust. It may take a little while to find

the spiritual prescription that suits you best, but if you want it
you will discover it!

For many years now, I have gone into my office early so I can
have time with God before the working day begins. This is the
only way I can enforce a spiritual discipline upon myself. I have
always found this is a good time for me to work on my journal.
You, too, might find it helpful to make space for yourself and for
God at the beginning of your day.

If you are not at ease with God first thing in the morning, then
try last thing at night. The evening is not much good for me, but
it suits some people far better. I have included some devotional
material at the end of this chapter, which you might find helpful
at the end of the day. Giving God some time as the day ends can
make all the difference in the world, for the giver of peace is able
to calm your natural fears and worries.

Perhaps you have never been comfortable with set prayers.
Don't be put off by them. They are an accumulation of treasures
the devout have used to talk with God down through the
centuries, and can become a springboard into the heart of heaven.
When anxious, often I find it difficult to know precisely what to
pray. During times like these, I turn to the words others have
used in their daily conversations with God and allowed them to
speak for me. Formal prayers are not the only way to talk with
the Almighty, but they have the ability to start the ball rolling. If
you play a musical instrument, you will know how important it
is to master your scales so you can be ready to play something
more creative. Set prayers are like intercessory scales. They can
get your prayer life off ground zero. Through them, you will
often find your conversation with God naturally moves onto a
more personal, intimate level.

Your journal is also part of your spiritual discipline.
Journaling can become like praying on paper. If your worries are
making concentration difficult, then write your prayers out in
your journal or diary. This is one of the best ways I know to keep
myself praying, especially if the petitions are interspersed with

a list of "to do's," schedules, thoughts on a conversation or interview, and problems arising from a tricky situation.

Physical Fitness

After years of physical idleness, my overweight and underexercised brother joined a health club when things were going badly in his business. This has revolutionized his life, turning him into a healthy fitness fanatic. These days, he's much fitter than I am! Where there were once rolls of flab, today there is muscle. His alcohol consumption has dropped, and I am certain his fitness has enabled him to withstand the stresses of the extraordinarily difficult business conditions that have prevailed in Britain for several years.

I am not necessarily suggesting you spend a fortune joining a gym, but I would encourage you to do something that will make your heart pound, your muscles stretch, and your pores sweat! If you don't want to work out or go jogging, then why not take long, brisk walks? Walking is good for you, and it doesn't cost a penny!

Because a job hunt is emotionally, spiritually, and intellectually demanding, it is easy to overlook the need for physical activity. But it is vital to your search that you stay physically fit, so commit yourself to some sort of exercise regimen.

A job hunt is also a time when you are tempted to drink or eat too much. Some people are natural nibblers when worried. A potato chip here, a cookie there, a candy bar in the middle of the afternoon, and before you know it you have added substantially to your intake without increasing the exercise necessary to burn these calories off. When your clothes don't fit and you can't afford new ones, you feel bad about yourself and a free fall begins in your self-esteem. This is not good for your job search.

Rake leaves, walk the dog, clean windows, dig the garden, mow the lawn, do *anything* that keeps you active. A former colleague's husband remodeled the kitchen and built a cabin in their backyard when he was between situations! If you enjoy walking, jogging, swimming, aerobics, or any other kind of exercise regimen, then go to it.

One of my favorite figures in American history is the great preacher and second president of Princeton University, Jonathan Edwards. As a Massachusetts pastor in the 1730s he spent hours each day in his study, preparing his sermons, praying, and counseling his flock. However, each afternoon he would strip off shirt and jacket and cut down trees and split wood for the stove his wife cooked on and to keep the house warm in the winter. I suspect he would have lived to a ripe old age if smallpox hadn't felled him soon after he moved from the edge of the Berkshires to urban Princeton, New Jersey.

Don't Despise Discipline

Discipline might not be a fashionable concept at the end of the twentieth century, but it is vital that we learn how to be disciplined if we are to get things done. Determination is essential if we are to succeed with anything, not least the identification of a new job. Without doubt, it is harder to impose discipline upon ourselves than it is to make a dozen people do our bidding.

This chapter is little more than a set of clues, giving you an idea of some of the things that are vital if you are to run a successful job search campaign. I do not have a lot of patience with ideas such as "Find a Better Job in Thirty Days," or "Better Pay for Fewer Hours—Finding a Job You'll Be Proud Of." You can be sure that such material can be really misleading, raising your expectations but delivering little. Their writers want you to feel good about yourself, which is fine, but they don't tell you enough about the "sweat equity" you need to put into your job search.

A job hunt is demanding, requiring both order and perseverance. But I promise that if you go about your search energetically, you will have deepened your inner resources by the time you are back in employment. So get out there and make those calls, pray those prayers, and watch the way such a disciplined approach will permanently change your life for the better.

Lord, we do not know how much of life
  is left to us in this world,
for you have veiled the future
  from our eyes.
But we know that all our days are in your hand
  and that no one can snatch us from your keeping.
Your mercy has never failed us throughout our life,
  nor will it fail us at the end.
So as we praise you for all that is past,
  we trust you for all that's to come,
in the name of our Saviour Jesus Christ.

Sunshine and shadow

God our Father, we live in a world of sunshine and shadow. Help us to accept that fact and not to expect life to be all sunshine.

May we remember that the sun is still shining even when we cannot see its light, and that it is the sunlight that creates the shadows.

So may we know that your love, like the sunshine, is unceasing and unchanging, and learn to trust you in life's darker hours as well as in the light; for Jesus' sake.

In anxiety and uncertainty

O God, you know how worried and anxious we are at this time about . . .

Help us to be calm and unflustered, and keep us trustful. When we have done all that is in our power, enable us to be patient and to leave the rest to you.

Above all, give us the certainty that you are with us in our trouble, that we may know your peace which the world cannot give and can never take away; for your love's sake. Heavenly Father, you know us better than we know our-selves,
so we need not tell you how perplexed we are.
Human advice often seems so shallow,
and we don't know what to do.
Help us to see our present situation through your eyes
and to relate it to your wider purposes.
Keep us from worrying over trivialities;
show us step by step what to do next;
and strengthen our faith in your ability
ultimately to bring good out of all that happens.
In Christ's name we ask it.

Waiting

God our Father, it is hard to wait. I realize that much of life is taken up with those "in-between" periods, waiting for something to happen, waiting for news, waiting for the letter that never seems to come. And now here I am, waiting again.

May this waiting period strengthen me as a person.

May your friendship and love transform this from being an empty experience without meaning into one of purpose and growth.

May I look back one day, grateful that I found in you the motivation and the power—to wait.

CHAPTER
NINE

HANDLING DISAPPOINTMENT

The interview goes well; your spirits are up. You leave for home feeling so good about yourself you start to daydream about what you're going to say when they offer you the job. By the time you walk through your own front door it feels as if the job is already yours. You settle down to wait for the phone to ring, comfortable in the knowledge that no one could be better placed for that position than you.

The days pass, and you hear nothing. You try to brush aside clouds of doubt and, in true American fashion, accentuate the positive. Perhaps you have already let other job searching slide. "They should have made up their minds about that position by now," you think after several weeks on tenterhooks. Yet, still there is no word.

Those who interviewed you *have* made up their minds. Instead of that congratulatory phone call saying how delighted they would be if you would join their corporation, a form letter arrives thanking you for your willingness to participate in their process, de-da-de-da, and telling you someone else has accepted the position. Some "Dear John" letters are even more disconcerting. So fulsome are they in their praise of the successful candidate that they make you feel an absolute nobody. I've had a quiverful of letters like this in my life, and whether I was eager about the position or not, they always make me feel very lowly.

Your spirits take a nose dive. You knew there was competition, but you felt you had been led to believe you were out in front of the field with an excellent chance of being selected. Besides, this was the job you *really* wanted, and you know you would have done the work well. Castles in the sky dissolve and you deflate as wave after wave of disappointment washes over you. You feel as if you have been kicked while you're down. Your enthusiasm for starting over wanes. You don't want to put yourself in the same position of vulnerability again. All you want is to bury your head in the sand and forget about new beginnings.

None of us handles disappointment well. If you are anything like me, it makes you morose. I lose my temper very easily after I have been disappointed and want to isolate myself from anything and anyone likely to cause me further pain. Others stop sleeping and eating, while still others of us overindulge in food as we try to suffocate the gnawing distress. My wife tends to escape into a barren wasteland somewhere deep inside herself; my brother just gets very, very angry.

During the months I was writing this book, to my surprise I was invited to be a candidate in a job search for a position I had always dreamed about, but had thought was way beyond my reach. Given the way the invitation was proffered, I thought I had a reasonable chance of being selected, and so did those I turned to for counsel. I felt utterly disheartened when I went all the way through the process, only to learn I was not the successful applicant at the end of the day. I was forced to wrestle with the demons of self-doubt and disappointment. It took me a long time to get my life and expectations back onto an even keel again.

Be Prepared

When looking for work, like the proverbial Boy or Girl Scout, you need to "be prepared" for things to go wrong. To use good old-fashioned biblical language, you must have "your loins girded up" so you are ready to handle the "thanks, but no thanks" calls and letters when they come. Disappointments are an inevitable part of the job search landscape. Unless you are extremely fortunate, scenarios like the one I've described will endeavor to blow your search off course.

Part of the emotional hard work of a job search is coming to terms with the occasions when others, including potential employers, slam the door in your face. We need a support group to help us through the weeks and months of transition. There's nothing better than friends. A group at church or a "soul friend" is best able to grasp our inner turmoil, pick us up, dust us off, and point us in the right direction again.

> *Part of the emotional hard work of a job search is coming to terms with the occasion when others, including potential employers, slam the door in your face.*

None of us likes rejection. However, unless you are extremely fortunate, you can't escape it. Rejection is the flip side of the search for new employment. The agony that accompanies disappointments must not be allowed to obliterate your enthusiasm. It is imperative that you get the pieces of your shattered psyche into some kind of repair and quickly return to the trenches of the job market.

When disappointment happens and you find yourself feeling defeated, only you and God together can answer the question "Is this the beginning of the downward path to oblivion, or am I going to savor it, learn the lessons it has to teach me, and make it the first stepping-stone to victory?"

The Job Hunter as a Gumshoe!

A job hunt can best be described as a sleuthing exercise. Like a private eye or a modern-day Sherlock Holmes, it is inevitable that you will at times find yourself following false trails in the process of finding your way to the right job. You are bound to take a few wrong turns. There will be times when you will be convinced you are going in the right direction when actually you are following a red herring. You need to think of a job search as a process of slowly paring down the alternatives. Sometimes it is particularly difficult to identify the true from the erroneous, particularly in the early stages of the hunt. At that point, there just aren't enough clues to go on. When I found myself a candidate for that dream job last year, if I had known then some of the things I know now, I would not have allowed my hopes to be raised as high as they were.

As you sleuth your way to a new position, you are looking at opportunities, using your best judgment to assess them, and acting on that judgment. This is an artform, not a precise science. So when you are wrong, you are forced to reassess the situation and then program into your search the necessary course corrections.

It would be gratuitous for me to go into all the gory details of the mental anguish associated with disappointment. You have probably had more than your fair share of it already and know exactly what it feels like. While such distress does have the ability to stop you dead in your tracks, you have to work hard to prevent it from diverting you from the important business of looking for new work. This chapter is a series of clues to help you deal with disappointment, then press on.

Willpower

First and foremost, there is no substitute for just keeping going. Okay, you might allow yourself to luxuriate in your misery for a day or two; but for goodness' sake, don't allow yourself to drown in it. I know this is easy to say and difficult to do, but the longer you wallow in your distress, the harder you are making it for yourself to get back on track.

You can play the "If only . . . " game forever. Wishful thinking and dreaming about what might have been don't get you back into the work force as a productive member of society. Too many of us tend to bask in feeling sorry for ourselves at precisely that moment when we should be pulling ourselves together, redoubling our efforts, and getting back into the fray.

I grew up in Britain in the bleak years following World War II, years that were to the English what the 1930s were to Americans. From a very early age, all of us had to grit our teeth and just keep going. Everywhere we looked, there was a nation painfully putting itself back together after six years of devastation. We were often told the story of King Robert the Bruce of Scotland.

Robert Bruce was a medieval king who had been trounced by the English at the Battle of Bannockburn. Having watched his army scatter to the four winds, the king is said to have fled for his life, finally taking refuge in a remote cave. There he foundered in his misery, despairing for the future of his country and blaming himself for their defeat. Scotland was lost—and it was his fault.

His only companion was a spider that was struggling to drape its web across the ceiling. Time and again, despite gargantuan efforts, it failed to sling in place the strategic threads on which to anchor its creation. Exhausted but undaunted, the spider did not give up. It would regroup, then try different tactics, until finally, after seemingly impossible efforts, the web was in place.

Observing the extraordinary efforts of his tiny companion, the beaten king took heart. "If a spider can rescue victory from the jaws of defeat, why not a king?" he thought to himself. So psychologically and spiritually he refocused himself, then went out and rallied his troops. Once more they met the English on the battlefield and proceeded to give them the trouncing of their lives! I say to you, learn the lesson of King Robert the Bruce and his spider.

No one has promised that finding a new job will be easy, but you won't find one at all if you don't keep your eyes on the prize.

Don't Personalize Rejection

One of the reasons I handle rejection badly is that I tend to personalize it. I want to make it my fault that I was passed over. While it is true that occasionally the main reason I might be rejected is because I'm me, a variety of other valid reasons applies as well. The person who got the position I was invited to apply for last year has proved to be far and away the best candidate for the job.

In most instances when you are rejected, the reason may be as simple as the successful candidate being better qualified. Those doing the interviewing and selection have weighed what they perceived to be your abilities against those of other contenders and made a cut. They made their decision not because you are useless, but because they sincerely believed someone else was better suited to that situation.

My present work demands that I spend much of my time fund-raising for our agency. Seldom does a day or two pass when I don't have to ask someone to make a donation to our cause. It is inevitable that people will turn down the opportunity to give more often than they say yes. They aren't rejecting me because I am who I am. They are saying no because they don't have the funds, or because what we do does not fit their financial priorities. The decision is theirs. I cannot make their judgments for them, but I do have to live with the consequences of their decisions.

The same is true when you are turned down for a position you thought you could fill well. Personalize it, and you're making a whip for your own back or are incubating a whole bed of ulcers that will eat through your insides. Life is much too short to spend all of it moping over what might have been. Even in the toughest job market you can be certain there are more opportunities where that one came from, even if it doesn't seem like it at the moment.

Don't Panic

I don't think there is anything worse than watching your reserves dwindle while the means to improve the situation—a steady job—remains mysteriously elusive. You wake up in the middle of the night, worrying about what will become of you. In the darkness, you feel a great tidal wave of panic wash over you. Unless you are able to keep a tight grip on yourself, you are likely to be swept away.

Keeping a clear head is one of the highest priorities when on a job search. As soon as you allow panic to take the wheel, you stop thinking straight and are prone to irrationality. When this happens, you are bound to generate significantly more heat than light, sometimes harming your job prospects. An interviewer can usually identify such agitation. You come across badly and do damage to your cause.

One way to minimize panic is to develop a clear strategy for finding new work early on in your search. Perhaps your strategy should be coupled with time lines. Set target dates by which certain things should be done. Obviously such a strategy needs to be regularly reviewed and treated with a measure of flexibility.

If you have in place a framework around which to build your campaign, then you will have a structure that will help you fend off panic and the pangs of disappointment. Any number of job hunting manuals spell out guidelines about developing such a strategy.[1] If you have had any experience in planning as part of your previous jobs, then you probably already have a fine professional skill that can help you in a personal situation like this.

---

1. See the "To Help You in Your Search" section for resources that I recommend.

Alongside such practical considerations, put your Christian faith. This is where it can be a real comfort. When everything looks as if it is falling apart, remember that "underneath are the everlasting arms." God's ways are not always easy to understand, so it may feel as if the Almighty is a million miles away when we are in the midst of trials and tribulations. But when we look back later, we are often able to see how God guided us as we wove our way through the shoals and quicksands of misfortune. At the end of this chapter, I have included some prayers you might find helpful when you are fraught with panic.

Avoid Paralysis

The child of panic is paralysis. It can develop gradually or strike with the suddenness of a bolt of lightning. When you are feeling miserable, you don't want to make those necessary phone calls, visit persons who might help you, build your network, write letters, or fill out the necessary job applications. But becoming a couch potato will not spirit a new job out of thin air. Remember our journalist friend in London from an earlier chapter, and how hard he had to work at finding his new position.

Overcoming paralysis may take what seems like a superhuman effort, but it is worth it. This is the place of willpower. The "how-to" books on career transition often underestimate how long it is going to take to find a new position. The search often requires the stamina of a long-distance runner. The difference about this race and running a marathon is that in this situation you are not quite sure when you will cross the finish line.

Disappointments are obstacles on the course. Your task is to make sure they don't eliminate you from the competition completely. Sitting at home and pitying yourself is not going to generate respect from potential employers. Pity is not the stuff of which job offers are made. You would not be human if you didn't have a cry or get angry when things don't seem to be going right; but when you are disappointed, it is critical to keep moving ahead.

A Listening Ear

The circumstances in which you now find yourself mean that you need a job support group—family, friends, pastor—to encourage and affirm you. Few of us are strong enough to get through a job search on our own, and it would be foolish bravado for any of us to try to do such a thing.

Talking through your feelings with your pastor or someone you trust who can offer a listening ear is essential. If you have a good relationship with your pastor, you might find it helpful to make a regular appointment to chat with him or her about your situation and prospects as your search develops. You will probably find that input from such sources will inevitably blow away some of the clouds of paralysis, as well as help you put your woes and disappointments into perspective. A Christian counselor can also help bring facets of the faith to bear upon your dilemma. There are any number of psalms in the Old Testament that were written at times of important change in the authors' lives. Turn to them for encouragement.

Be Positive

Finally, attempt to cultivate a positive outlook through this difficult period of your life. While you might not be able to eliminate the negative entirely, the more despairing your outlook, the more difficult it will be to present yourself vivaciously and as an attractive candidate for a career opportunity.

This means listening carefully to your innermost thoughts. Attempt to monitor what your mind is saying to you. When you hear negative, despairing thoughts, try to separate reality from what someone has called "catastrophizing." Catastrophizing is when we turn every setback and every difficulty into a momentous problem that we are convinced will wipe us out.

The late 1980s and early 1990s have not been easy years for small, nonprofit organizations like the one I direct. As the nation went to war in the Middle East, as recession made individuals much more cautious in their charitable giving, and as Christian congregations were forced to cut back outreach giving in an attempt to shore up massive deficit budgets, there have been times when I have found myself wondering whether we would make it.

On one occasion, when things were particularly grim, I lost grip of myself in a meeting and allowed myself to catastrophize. Immediately, one of my trustees took me aside and very graciously gave me a serious talking to. Then he gave me good advice about not allowing my deepest worries to take control. If you are to retain a positive outlook, then trusted companions for the journey to a new job are vital.

It Will Turn Out All Right in the End

Several years ago I was in New Mexico visiting with a man who had been through an extended period of unemployment. Through no fault of his own, he had many strikes against him, and I, for one, thought he was going to be left high and dry. He was prepared to wait a long time to get the position he now holds. He did not allow a steady flow of rejections to squeeze the life out of his motivation, and neither did he panic when financial stringencies made it necessary for the family to tighten their belts. Instead, he continued to nurture his network until the perfect job came along.

On a chilly March day we stood on a hillside overlooking Santa Fe. "I couldn't imagine living and working in a more beautiful place," my friend told me. He's right—and out of a string of disappointments has come a career into which he can enthusiastically throw his whole weight.

I hope the same is true for you before very long.

For ourselves

>   Be silent
>   still
>   aware
>   for there
>   in your own heart
>   the Spirit is at prayer
>   listen and learn
>   open and find
>   heart-wisdom
>   Christ.

(Prayer from Malling Abbey, a House of Anglican Benedictine Nuns.)

TEN

JOB HUNTING IS A SPIRITUAL JOURNEY

It was in the desert . . . that the people of Israel learned the lesson of dependence upon God in the simplicity of pure faith.
Kenneth Leech, *Spirituality and Pastoral Care*

The Footsteps in the Sand

A few days before I sat down to write this chapter, I found myself on business in Princeton, New Jersey. One of the most pleasant aspects of that glorious spring visit was a delightful hour spent drinking coffee and chatting with George S. Gallup, Jr., the noted pollster and public opinion surveyor, a man whom I've really gotten to know in the last few years. As we talked about some of the work he was doing at that moment, he threw out a thought that has haunted me ever since.

"Our surveys," he told me, "are increasingly suggesting that Americans are some of the loneliest people in the world."

Much to the disgust of the rest of my family, I am a very early riser. I had been up for hours before my morning appointment with George in his office on a quiet street a short stone's throw from Princeton University, and had spent the time reworking the manuscript of this then unfinished book. As I scanned the pages, I had been startled by the number of times I have mentioned that searching for a new job is ultimately a one-person business, and how very lonely it can be. Now here was a man with his finger on the pulse of American society, telling me that one of our national characteristics is that many of us go through extended periods of desperate loneliness.

I spent much of the next forty-eight hours behind the wheel of my car, a place where I do a lot of my thinking. As I drove, I found myself returning to George Gallup's thought again and again. Job searching is, as I have said already, a one-person task, so it is obvious that being out of work is going to intensify this sense of being on your own. I found myself wondering how this fed into the increased sense of loneliness that many Americans feel.

When I arrived home, there on my desk with the rest of my mail was a complimentary copy of a book about prayer. After glancing through my letters, I turned to the book and casually thumbed through its pages. Well-written and nicely presented, it seemed to cover all the important points, but the book did little to fire my imagination. That is, until my eye caught a rather sentimental, but extremely effective, little parable. I had probably heard it a thousand times before, but this author had found a powerful way of giving the story new breadth and poignancy.

One night a man had a dream. He dreamed he was walking along the beach with the Lord. Across the sky flashed scenes from his life. For each scene he noticed two sets of footprints in the sand. He noticed that many times along the path of his life there was only one set of footprints. He also noticed that it happened at the very lowest and saddest times of his life. This really bothered him and he questioned the Lord about it. "Lord, you said that once I decided to follow you, you would walk with me all the way. But I have noticed that during the most troublesome times of my life, there is only one set of footprints. I do not understand why, when I needed you most you would leave me." The Lord replied, "My precious, precious child! I love you and would never leave you. During your times of trial and suffering, when you see only one set of footprints, it was then that I carried you."

Lonely, But Not Alone

Yes, a job search is likely to be one of the loneliest periods of your life, but the Christian message assures us that as empty and friendless as we might feel, we are never out of the presence of God. Even if the Lord seems very distant from you at this precise moment, Christ is your companion. Right now, if you were able to look at things from beyond the perspective of time, you would likely turn around and find just one, not two sets of footsteps in the sands of time.

The Christian life is full of apparent ambiguities—that's what makes the faith so difficult for some people to understand. This is why it is often called a mystery. One such oddity is that the most profound spiritual changes often take place when we are least aware of them. Sometimes the most painful times are the times of greatest spiritual growth. Even if times are hard and God seems distant, he has not left us to stew in our own juice. The Almighty enables us to surmount obstacles—internal ones, as well as the stumbling blocks that life sometimes throws in our way. At this moment, you may feel very alone, but God is not going to drop you or let you go, even if at times, from your perspective, it looks as if your whole life is in the process of being flushed down the toilet!

In the midst of the greatest time of crisis in my life, feeling like a beached whale, I groaned one day to a priest who was trying to help me that I wished all this would end and I could get back to living. He looked me squarely in the eyes and said, "Richard, you are probably doing more living now than you have ever done in your life before." It seemed a cruel comment at the time, but subsequently, I have discovered he was right. As agonizing as that period of my life had been, it was one that has shaped my whole future.

Perhaps it would have been better if the anonymous composer of that little parable had dreamed about walking through a sandy desert rather than along a beach. Beaches are places many of us associate with pleasure, but hard times have traditionally been considered wilderness experiences; it is as if our skin is scorched by the blazing sun and our throats are permanently dry. Persons in such arid states are not going to compose sweet conversations with God about the niceties of life; they are going to be gasping, "Water . . . water . . . give me some water!"

When we find ourselves caught between this rock and the hard place, our prayers will often be peppered with agonized pleas. They are full of passion and yearning, and there's no reason why they should be put together in the most perfect English. They are more likely to be groans and gasps than a series of well-constructed phrases and sublime thoughts.

> *The most profound spiritual changes often take place when we are least aware of them.*

"Please, Lord," we pray, "get me out of this mess and help me find a good job." Such a prayer doesn't have the cadence of the Episcopal Church's *Book of Common Prayer* or the King James Version of the Bible, but it is genuine and heartfelt, coming straight from the soul—or if you prefer it, the gut. It is an expression of our deep need for God as we navigate through the stones and brambles of this barren chapter of life. If you are praying, and I'm sure you are, I suspect your prayers are more likely to be of this kind.

Let me reassure you that such intercessions are neither cheap nor second rate. Praying is being in a conversation with God in the same way you would talk to your parents, your spouse, or your closest friends and confidants. Even if your mother is a professor of English literature, you don't arrange perfect sentences in your mind before pouring out your soul to her, making sure each phrase or clause is properly constructed. Neither is this necessary with God. The Lord God Almighty invites us, his children, to call him "Abba," which is the ancient Aramaic word for "Daddy." "Because you are children, God has sent the Spirit of his Son into our hearts, crying, 'Abba! Father!' " (Gal. 4:6). This gives us the clue that prayers should be personal and intimate.

The reason I have included a wide selection of prayers and devotionals throughout this book is that I hope you will be able to use them during this stressful period of your life. It is always helpful to have a springboard to get you into the business of praying. That is one of the reasons I have supplemented the text in this way. These prayers are there to get you started, or, at least, to help you find a few words to say to God when words don't seem all that willing to form in your mind. Many people find that once their spiritual pump has been primed in this way, it isn't too difficult to talk very naturally to the Almighty.

I used to enjoy dropping by to see a well-known writer who lived in the same town that I did. Very early in our friendship, I discovered how important it was to have three or four topics prepared in my mind, because this woman found conversation rather difficult until she'd had a chance to warm up. Once she was primed, we would have a stimulating talk, but for some mysterious reason she needed help getting started! Praying can be very much like this, so I commend these prayers to you to start the ball rolling.

Writing Down Your Prayers and Shooting Arrows

If getting started in prayer is still difficult for you, then try writing your thoughts down. In an earlier chapter, we talked about keeping a journal of your job hunt. As I suggested there, I find my journal is not only a good way to think through the joys and challenges that are shaping my life, but I also use it as an aid to prayer. As I look back through my growing accumulation of journals, I notice that a significant percentage of the material recorded is actually my praying.

I find it difficult to keep my mind on a particular subject for more than a few seconds when praying, so the discipline of putting my prayers into writing enables me to stay focused. I don't write in perfect English. I just allow my thoughts to become prayers and then flow straight from the tip of my pen. This is something you might try if you decide to use a journal to help you in your job search.

Then there are those little "arrow prayers" that you can shoot heavenward when you don't have the time or are not in the right place to devote a significant chunk of time to the business of being in touch with God. Perhaps you are on your way to an interview, the butterflies are out of control in your stomach, and you are waiting at a traffic signal that stays red for an interminable time. Why not use that moment to shoot your request to God in prayer? Something like, "O God, I'm feeling awful and need your help as I go to this interview. You know what's best for me. May things work out according to your will."

Obviously, there's a lot more to prayer than what I've said here. Some people I know have found that the experience of joblessness whets their appetite to understand prayer better, and then to pray more effectively. If that is so with you, I'm sure a Christian bookstore or your pastor will be able to guide you. In even the humblest congregation there are usually two or three people who know how to pray in depth and can help others with their intercessory life. Your pastor can put you in touch with these folks and show you the books you might find helpful as you set out to deepen your spiritual journey.

Let God Talk to You

So far, I've only talked about prayer as your communicating with God, but it is in fact a two-way conversation. You need to listen for God's response. Whenever I read something like the words I've just written, it sounds to me a little out of touch with reality. Yet, as I have discovered so many times, God talks to us in both ordinary and extraordinary ways.

I've been a practicing Christian now for more than thirty years, but I've never yet heard voices or seen something supernatural. When God talks to me, it is usually through a verse of Scripture, the way a set of circumstances come together and work out, or through the counsel of a wise friend or mentor to whom I have turned for help. Often it might be a series of coincidences that combine to nudge me in the right direction. I've spent a lifetime learning to discern which of these whispers is the voice of God prompting me. I am still learning.

A few days ago, I was talking to a friend on the phone. He is just about to start a new job about which he is quite anxious. It is probably the most demanding thing he has ever done in his life. He was sharing some of his misgivings about uprooting his family, moving halfway across the country, then taking on the thankless task of clearing up the accumulated debris of years of poor management and bad human relationships. Just when I was feeling depressed for him as he girded himself up to walk into this lions' den, the conversation brightened and he said, "But the other morning I was reading the Bible, and this verse jumped off the page at me."

Over the phone he quoted that piece of Scripture to me. Each of us had probably read it countless times before, but on this occasion it seemed to be particularly comforting and illuminating to him. From his perspective, this was God talking directly to him, assuring him that everything would be all right. Coincidence, perhaps, but as someone once said, when you stop praying, the coincidences stop happening.

Prayer is the means our Creator has provided for us to get close to him, and make ourselves available to him, and himself accessible to us. It is not some magic wand you can wave to make the Almighty do your bidding; rather, it is a God-given means of tuning in to his plan for our lives. While you must not expect God to show you more than one step of the journey ahead of you at a time, eventually you will be able to turn around, look back, and see your whole life has actually been shaped and patterned by God.

When Bad Things Happen to Good People

Following the death of his son, Harold Kushner sat down with his pen and tried to find the meaning behind this appalling tragedy that had darkened his life and shaken his image of God. The result was a book entitled *When Bad Things Happen to Good People*. It was a brave book, beautifully written, and deservedly spent many months on the *New York Times* best-seller list.

It sold so well because Rabbi Kushner's words struck a chord with literally millions of Americans—Christians, Jews, Moslems, and even people of no faith at all. They saw their personal struggles in the pages he had written, and with him were eager to go on an expedition of discovery, which might make sense of the variety of unjust mishaps that had blighted their lives. For millennia, sages and ordinary folks have sought answers for the almost unanswerable question, "Why did *this* have to happen to *me*? I really don't think I deserve it!"

Perhaps you have been saying things like this, or thinking along these lines. Why did *I* have to lose my job? Why did this have to happen when it did? I was the one who did all the creative work in that office, yet it was she who stayed and I was fired. This really isn't fair at all. No, it usually isn't, and despite our best efforts we are ever only half able to make sense of our demise.

However, our relationship with God, charged and edified through our prayers, helps us to cope with the injustices and inconsistencies of life. It also enables us to delve beneath the surface of this tragedy and, even if we cannot understand it, recognize that it is during troublesome episodes, like being without work, that we are enabled to grow in grace and Christian maturity.

Sometimes the presence of God is very real and obvious. It is as if we can reach out and touch him. At other times, God seems distant, veiled, hidden from our eyes. But despite how we feel, God is always there, and always immediately available to us. Prayer is the means whereby we engage our lives with God, and discover where he is leading and guiding. You can be certain as you continue to seek God's will that there will be surprises—but wouldn't life be incredibly dull if there weren't these unexpected twists and turns in the road?

In a job hunt, the agony and the ecstasy go hand in hand. Perhaps today you are feeling the agony, whereas tomorrow the logjam of possibilities will break and the ecstasy will surge through your being. God's hand is in all you do and all you experience. Look for God to guide you forward until you are at the place God wants you to be.

Arrow prayers

Lord Jesus Christ, Son of God,
be merciful to me, a sinner.
(The Jesus Prayer)

Dear God, be good to me:
the sea is so wide and my boat is so small.
(Prayer of Bréton fishermen)

Lord, you have given so much to me: give me one thing more, a grateful heart.
(After George Herbert)

Let my chief end, O God, be to glorify you, and to enjoy you for ever.
(From the Shorter Catechism)

CHAPTER
ELEVEN

SO YOUR SPOUSE IS JOB HUNTING. . .

For husband and wife
Heavenly Father,
Marriage is of your making.
It is you who have joined us together
  as man and wife.
We pray that throughout our married life
  you will give us grace at all times
    to be true to one another,
    to consider one another's needs,
    to support one another in trouble,
    to forgive one another's mistakes,
    to love one another to the end.
So may we as man and wife enjoy your constant
  blessing and live together for your glory.

Although Pursued Alone, Job Hunting Involves the Whole Family

When the rubber hits the road, job hunting is a one-person task that involves every member of the family.[1] Everyone is unsettled

---

1. This chapter is designed for the partners of those looking for work, but job hunters should read, learn, and inwardly digest it themselves.

by the upheaval of one of the breadwinners' being out of work, especially if it looks as if a new position will involve moving to another city, another state, or in an increasing number of instances, another country.

The individual most able to help you, but at the same time most likely to be troubled by your search for a fresh start, is likely to be your spouse. This chapter is designed to be shared with your life partner. I've written it in the form of a letter to your nearest and dearest, because that seemed the easiest way to get across difficult information. If you are married, I hope you will feel free to share it with your spouse. If you are single, then a parent, sibling, child, close friend, or support group might find the letter helpful.

> *Job hunting is a one-person task that involves every member of the family.*

Although I have designed the letter as if I were writing to the wife of an unemployed man, feel free to switch names around and address the missive to a male. In today's job market, Jim is increasingly likely to be the spouse trying to cope with his wife's employment misfortunes. Make an effort to see how my words and your family situation might intersect.

Dear Carol:

Your anxiety jumped down the phone at me when we talked the other evening. With Jim being laid off like that, I realize how terribly worried you must be. I've talked with so many folks who have experienced something similar in the last few years; while they know they are not unique, it is very easy to feel terribly isolated as you set out toward a new and sometimes frightening future. You don't know where you're going to be living or what

Jim's work will be a few months from now—such uncertainty takes the shine from the adventure.

I know it must be particularly distressing when you have watched your spouse do the best job he could, and nevertheless get thrown out of work in the twinkling of an eye, because he was excess to requirements at that moment. I agree with you that there is something extraordinarily cruel about a world in which a person is judged by the impact he or she makes on the balance sheet, but you have to remember that every corporation today is learning how to be lean and mean in a very tough, competitive situation.

Try to look at your circumstance differently. Instead of viewing it as an unmitigated disaster, have you thought that Jim's former employer might suddenly have dropped into your lap the most splendid opportunity, the opportunity of a lifetime? I called it an adventure in my first paragraph, and I don't shy away from that word now.

If you were my wife, by this point you would be getting angry and telling me that I sound more like Pollyanna than someone whose feet are firmly planted on the ground. Don't get me wrong; I'm not insensitive to your misery, but give some thought to your circumstances. You have been given a wonderful chance that job security might have hidden from many others; that is, to ask fundamental questions about what you want to do with the rest of your lives.

I can't promise the butterflies will tone down that ball they are probably having in your stomach, or that you will sleep more soundly through the night, but I can promise that as you start looking at this as an opportunity, the color of the sky might start to turn from an overcast gray to a more friendly shade of blue. You will weep, wail, and gnash your teeth, and if you are normal you will find yourself wondering if this nightmare will ever end. But, approached expectantly, knowing that you are not beyond God's reach, rebuilding can be a stimulating adventure, even if you are not sure *what* waits around the next corner.

Many Christians call this adventure "living by faith." You, Jim, and your family are like Abraham setting out from the civilized and fertile Ur of the Chaldees, journeying into the unknown. You don't know where God is leading, but you do know there is a "Promised Land" at the end of the trail. "Faith," the Bible tells us, "is the assurance of things hoped for, the conviction of things not seen" (Heb. 11:1). You are traveling outward in faith, trying to see where the Lord might lead you.

Let me be brutally frank: Unless Jim is extremely lucky, this hiatus is going to go on for several months. There will be days when it will seem to you as if his job search is going nowhere, and I am sure you will be tempted to get on his case. The whole situation is likely to put strains on your marriage, and you need to monitor that. Yet cling to this hope: There is a light on at the end of the tunnel, and each new day is bringing you one step closer to it. Things would have to be very, very bad indeed in this topsy-turvy economy for anyone to have turned that light off!

I cannot stress the importance of your role as a supportive spouse in this whole process. The way you handle things could make the difference between Jim's rushing into something new that is not right for him, thereby backing himself into a dead-end position, or making an exciting career move that will bring both of you happiness and fulfillment. Too many people I know have taken the first job offer to come down the pike in order to ease their spouse's anxieties, only to discover a few months later that had they waited just a little longer they would not have missed the proverbial "big one."

Your mission on this journey into the unknown is to be Jim's best friend, confidante, cheerleader, and most constructive critic. When someone loses his or her work it is entirely natural for that person to start imagining he or she is worthless and that life now has little value. Men, in particular, but an increasing number of women, have a tendency to wrap up their whole identity in their work, turning it into an idol at whose shrine they worship morning, noon, and night. To suddenly have that false god taken away can be a rude awakening. If this is Jim, then please try to help him out of this crevasse as only you can. When you married him you vowed it would be "for better or for worse." Now is a moment when he is calling on you to stand by your pledge—he needs you now as never before.

The loss of a job is like a death in the family. As you know, someone who is bereaved experiences the whole gamut of emotions. Think of yourselves as the loved ones of the deceased. It is important not only that you mourn the loss yourself, but also that you give Jim "permission" to grieve over his loss. As he mourns, you should be thinking of ways in which you can provide a secure setting within which he can regroup. If you're puzzled how to go about this, why not make an appointment to have a chat with your pastor?

For a while, the first few weeks at least, the onus for family life and your daily routine is likely to fall on your shoulders. Try to keep things at home as normal as possible. Rise at the usual time and make sure Jim gets up, too; keep the house clean; eat family meals together; and maintain the sort of pattern that has been normal in your household. When a crisis hits, the fewer surprises a shell-shocked person has to face the better. And when you set off for work, make sure Jim has a schedule for the day that includes plenty of job search activities.

Cheerleading

You may not have been a pom-pon girl when you were at school, but now I'm asking you to be Jim's number-one cheer-leader. While his morale is so low that he feels as if life is passing him by, it is more than likely he will prevaricate about getting back into the job market. It is not unusual for a normally responsible person to attempt to hide away from a predicament like this and pretend it is not there, unless there is someone lovingly encouraging him along. Like a wild animal that has lost a fight, he is hiding away in order to lick his wounds.

You can help him best not only by jollying him along, but by encouraging him to set goals for each day. Perhaps you can get into the habit of sitting down together each evening to review what he has achieved, work out how many phone calls he will make tomorrow, who he will visit, and how many hours he will spend on journaling or building his résumé. Then when the next evening rolls around you will be there to assess the day's progress and, perhaps, setbacks, and in the light of these make suggestions for the next day's job hunting strategy. And remember the old 12-Step program slogan, a job search is "one day at a time."

A Shoulder to Cry On

One of the hard things about a job search is just keeping going. Put crudely, Jim's task at the present is to see himself as a product that he has to go out to market to potential employers. When they say, "No, thank you," he is likely to get downhearted. There is nothing unusual about this because if it is yourself that you are selling, rather than cornflakes or elegant evening shoes, then you are emotionally much more attached to the product and whether it succeeds or not. Even the toughest men and women in the world struggle with such apparent "rejection."

When Jim comes home from rebuffs like this, and there are bound to be a few of them, give him a shoulder to cry on and help him recharge his emotional batteries for the next day. Try to approach his situation from a positive direction. The people who said no might well have done him a favor, and God could very well have something far better a little further down the road.

Recently, without my going out and looking for it, I found myself a candidate for a job, the idea of which grew on me the more I thought about it. Eventually, the position was given to someone else, and I was left out in the cold. I felt rejected and was resentful because it seemed to me the successful candidate lacked the experience I would have brought to that work. Now I have had time to think about it and get over the initial sense of rejection. I realize with all the problems they were facing I was not the best person for the job and would very likely have messed things up. At first I was upset with God for letting this happen, but now I realize he actually acted in my best interests. Today, I can rejoice that I didn't get that position because there was still a lot to do in the job I already have, and I had missed it.

Keeping Him Focused and Faithful to Himself

If Jim is to have a successful job search, you must do all in your power to keep him focused on that task. Help him to be single-minded, and listen to him when he wants to talk. Of course, you should share your life with him, but try not to overload him with too many of your own problems at this difficult time. Love him, care for him, and do all you can to "psych" him up for his next foray into the job market.

Also, please remember that Jim is not only out looking for employment, but he is also searching for the right employer. Knowing him as well as you do, you are in the best position to debrief him following interviews, whether they are merely ranging shots or serious possibilities.

Every organization has its own personality. Some corporation might start looking serious at Jim, which as you listen to his descriptions of it, would be totally wrong for him—and, therefore, indirectly, for you as well. As the one who knows him best and who loves him, you can help him analyze the situation, and perhaps steer him away from settings where he would be miscast. But you can't make up his mind for him; you can only show him the pros and cons. It could cause terrible difficulties if you talked him out of something that might have been wonderful for him because you didn't like the sound of it. Obviously, it is far better if it is a shared decision.

Making Ends Meet

Jim would not be normal if he were not worrying about how you are going to make ends meet financially. During the next few months, frugality has to be the name of the game; but do your best to make it a game! Whatever you do to cut back expenditures, avoid making life gray and colorless. An occasional treat, however small, is a wonderful picker-upper.

See if you can find ways to spoil yourselves that aren't very costly. John Templeton is a man who, from humble beginnings in rural Tennessee, made a fortune on Wall Street, but at the start of his career he had nothing. In one of the books he has written about the spiritual side of that journey to success, he tells of the way he and his wife enjoyed themselves and ate out in the 1930s, even when they still had orange-crate furniture in their New York apartment. He tells his readers that part of the pleasure was the joy of the hunt for low-cost entertainment and eating places.

Recently some friends of mine experienced a significant drop in income. The temptation was to fall back on credit cards, but instead of falling into the debt trap they turned their family budget into a strictly cash economy. If they could not afford something, they did not buy it. It worked wonders and kept them solvent through a lean patch. Why not try something like that in your home?

Your Children

Then there's the kids. It is likely to be a baffling time for them, although the older one will have a better understanding of what's going on than the youngster. Wherever possible, try to include them in discussions, but remember there is just so much they are able to handle. I've noticed over the years that it is usually the need to cut back on family budgets that makes life the most difficult for kids, so I suggest you find ways of ameliorating that.

However, this "in-between time" is also a great opportunity for your daughter and son to spend more quality time with their father. While I cannot emphasize enough that job hunting is Jim's full-time occupation for the foreseeable future, the hours he puts in can be much more flexible than the standard office routine, and, besides, his office is now at home. It would probably be a mistake to turn him into "Mr. Mom," but he will certainly have chances to enjoy his children's company, getting to know them in new ways, which may never occur again.

The best part about my own awkward career transition was the time I was able to spend with my two daughters. I did not enjoy being between jobs at all, but I'm sure my relationship with our girls improved during those months because I was able to give them more of my time and attention. There were days when it seemed to be their love that kept me sane. They are independent young women now, but I do not regret that chance we were given to deepen our friendship and change the quality of our relationship.

Looking After Carol

Finally, yourself. I can't pretend that this is going to be a picnic, but there is always at least one silver lining in this particular cloud. Approached positively, you can make this time of transition an experience that will help you and Jim grow as persons and Christians. It could very well add a new richness to your marriage as you attempt to slay this dragon together.

You will be called upon to play many roles in these days ahead: wife, mother, and lover being the most obvious. But you will also have to find ways of keeping him from retreating from human company, working with folks who will support him, and helping him manage the search process efficiently. This will drain you, I'm sure, which means that you, too, will need support to help you when everything seems to be getting on top of you.

I am sure you have special confidantes whom you can call upon, even if they live hundreds of miles away. In this situation an occasional long-distance phone call is not a luxury you should cut from your budget—although by calling in the evenings and on weekends, you can keep costs down a little bit. Perhaps there are women you know well who have gone through something similar and are able to share your experience more deeply. Members of your church, perhaps?

A group of two or three people with whom you can meet for coffee occasionally, or perhaps with whom you pray, and who are there at the end of the phone for you is vital if you are not to be debilitated by this experience yourself. Look after your physical and emotional health, the most valuable treasures in the world as you and Jim face this time of transition together.

When you have chosen your friends, be as honest and as wholehearted with them as possible. This is not the time to "keep up appearances," especially with those you have chosen to trust. One of my friends was telling me about his most recent career transition recently, and I was sorry he skirted around the nastier details of his obviously awkward move. He was embarrassed by what had happened. Not only did I feel less able to support him, but he also robbed me of the chance to pray knowledgeably for him and his family.

Which brings me to your church. This is a time you really need it. If things are difficult, try to get your pastor or one of the leaders you trust involved with your family. Remember, the church is often one of the very best places to find contacts that will lead to new career opportunities for your husband.

Keep in touch. I will certainly be praying for you both. If there is anything I can do to help, don't hesitate to let me know. Your friend,

Richard

Richard

CHAPTER
TWELVE

HAPPILY EVER AFTER...?

WARNING! You might want to glance at this chapter when you are in your job search, but I suggest keep it "on ice," then read it with care once you have been offered—and have accepted—your new position.

Life May Not Be a Fairy Story,
but When You Succeed, Celebrate!

There is a wonderful old square near the heart of Copenhagen that is "presided" over by an exquisite statue of Hans Christian Andersen. I visited that glorious corner of Denmark on a perfect Scandinavian summer day—the sky was a cloudless pale blue, and happy children skipped around the cobbles at the old man's feet. It was as if one of the great storyteller's tales had come alive before my eyes. I was enchanted.

Nothing would give me more pleasure than to end this book with a generous flourish, saying that once you are back in employment, you and your family will, like the ugly duckling-turned-into-a-swan, and so many other characters in Andersen's tales, live happily ever after. Alas, as you have probably learned from your own experience already, in the real world things are never that neat and tidy! I would be the one telling fairy tales if I gave you the impression that once you have a new position sewn up, your troubles are all over. Obviously, this is not true.

Now you are setting out on a different kind of transition. One harrowing set of hurdles is behind you, but another obstacle course is only just beginning! You have probably learned a tremendous amount about the world, yourself, your community—and your God—during this time "between jobs." Yet in some respects this chapter-change is far from over. You are likely to spend a considerable time processing what you have been through, and what it has taught you.

Celebrate! You have a job!

It is nearly ten years since I went through my worst employment nightmare, and still I find breaking in on me new insights that have been incubating since that stumbling, frightening time. While I don't ever want to repeat a time like that again, I am constantly becoming aware of facets from that period that played a part in maturing me, and for which I must give thanks to God. I might have hated those cold gray months when I was living through almost constant misery, but they forced me to do a great deal of growing up. I don't know anyone who has been to this kind of hell and back who does not agree with me.

However, before going out and "unpacking" what has happened to you since you last had regular employment, rejoice and celebrate. You have a job; you probably have a starting date; you might even have signed a contract. Thank the Lord for his goodness, and do something special. Many people have the impression that the Christian faith is dour and parsimonious, frowning on joy and delight, but they are utterly wrong. In my experience, Christians are often the most joyful of people, usually because they have so much to be thankful for.

Whether your favorite celebration is a party with a few friends, a meal with your spouse, a day at the amusement park with your children, sailing your boat, or walking alone along an Appalachian ridge enjoying the beauties of nature—get out and do it! You've worked hard for this moment. Enjoy! You are about to get back to work. The struggle has paid off, the pressure is off for the moment, so tuck the rest of your worries into a recess of your mind for a day or two, and let your hair down. The writers of the Psalms would say, "Rejoice and be glad!"

For many of us, a job search is one of the bleakest times of our lives. When it is over, we are free to fling open the shutters, let the fresh air waft in, and breathe more easily. It is important that you take advantage of this interlude before the inevitable stresses of the new job begin to weigh you down.

Christianity may be concerned with the serious issues of life and death, but Jesus went to parties and enjoyed himself. He told stories about weddings, feasts and "killing the fatted calf," so there is no reason why we should not bask in our accomplishments and celebrate for a little while, because our Lord set us a good example.

Thanksgiving and Thanksliving

But in the midst of your celebration, try not to forget God. I confess that when I'm in a pickle, and I pray for the Lord to intervene and he answers those petitions, I tend to nod a word of thanks in his direction, then forget the part he played in showering these glorious blessings upon me.

While it might seem we are the only ones who have invested "sweat equity" in finding ourselves a new job, that is only because we find it hard not to look at it from the temporal perspective. We are unable to see the part the Lord has played behind the scenes: opening doors, putting the right people in our way at the right time, even moving the minds of the folks who hired us to recognize our qualifications and determine that our personality fits their organization well.

Like the parable of the footsteps in the sand, which we looked at in a previous chapter, from our present perspective it is hard to identify how much the Lord carried us through these trying times. Only in the eternal retrospect will we find out these facts for ourselves—and the discovery is likely to humble us.

At the end of this chapter I have included one of my favorite "thank you" prayers—the "General Thanksgiving" from the *Book of Common Prayer*. Written by a seventeenth-century English bishop, it has fueled the thanksgivings of millions of Christians all over the world for nearly 350 years. I committed the "General Thanksgiving"to memory when I was an undergraduate; and despite my failure to use it as often as I ought, it has stood me in good stead ever since. In it, we thank God for "creation, preservation, and all the blessings of this life." No supercomputer could ever enumerate all the blessings this life affords, but for you, among them is that job you will be starting soon.

Yet we should be doing more than just telling God how grateful we are that the pieces of our lives are coming together again. If, during this time out from work, we have experienced real growth, then we should start looking for ways to live our lives in a spirit of thankfulness from here on out. Words, even words addressed to God in prayer, can be awfully cheap, but actions seldom are. A great Christian of the Victorian era once said that our thanksgiving should lead to "thanksliving." This may sound corny, but like so many corny phrases it is very memorable.

Perhaps one of the things you might be thinking about as you celebrate God's goodness to you is how you might return thanks for the pieces coming together again. My elder daughter is a college student. It has not always been easy as she has grappled to find her way forward in the adult world, but she has been fortunate enough to have received encouragement and counsel from a retired businessman and his wife. When I wrote the man, an alumnus of her high school, to thank him for his kindness, he responded with a wonderful letter. It was a long epistle. He told me his own story, and the help he had received early on which has borne much fruit. Now he wanted to give back the blessings showered upon him with some interest, and had decided to help young people just starting out.

He hoped Olivia would experience great success. After that, he hoped she would remember his example and pass on to a generation yet unborn some of her blessings, seeds that could have been planted by him and his wife. His example is a grand illustration of turning thanksgiving into "thanksliving."

If you keep your eyes open you are bound to find all sorts of ways you can live out your life thankfully. In what is often a self-centered world, a little bit of selflessness can go a long way toward making a significant difference in another's life. Any number of people have probably helped you attain your goal of a new position. As well as sending them letters giving them your good news and your thanks, you might look for ways to emulate their generosity.

If you're not in a position to do something for someone else, then a financial gift is often a good way of demonstrating your gratitude to God for getting you through this period in your life. It was just such a gift from a couple who had been unemployed for ten months that played a part in altering my whole life, giving me wonderful opportunities, and eventually bringing me and my family very unexpectedly to the United States in 1976. They described it as a "thank offering" for God's goodness to them.

If your pastor has been helpful to you during these dark days, then perhaps now is the time to consider a gift to his/her discretionary fund to be used to help someone else in trouble. These days there is a steady procession of people with tremendous needs who visit clergy in their offices. A few dollars can often make a life or death difference to these folks who have fallen on hard times.

A Life of Stewardship and Continual Learning

The other afternoon I was talking to a former senior executive from a huge multinational conglomerate. After thirty years working for the same company, he had decided to take early retirement and was now preparing to do something completely different. When I asked him how his colleagues had viewed his course change, he told me that in general they were quite relieved. "These days few corporations want people hanging around on their payroll forever," he confided.

As we have seen already, there is no such thing today as lifetime employment. Depending on your age, your experience, and your new employer, it is a distinct possibility this new position will not be your last before retirement. Because of the nature of today's marketplace, America has, of necessity, become a society of job-hoppers. Whether we like it or not, most of us are destined to have several careers, and in addition, even more paid positions.

As we saw in the chapter "Change, Change, Change," work and the workplace are altering so rapidly and radically that the position you are about to take could have a lifespan of only a few years. Before you know it, it could evaporate before your eyes as newer technologies and opportunities come into play. Just recently, pollster George Barna pointed out that in the 1990s America is remaking itself every three to five years, and this applies to the work place every bit as much as it applies to our communities, schools, and family structures.

Buggy whip manufacturers thought the world was their oyster at the beginning of the century, so they looked with scorn on the dirty, smelly cars that were starting to appear on the roads. Mass production transformed motoring from a millionaire's hobby and put all of us, except perhaps the Amish, behind the wheel of an automobile. Within a generation almost all of the country's whip makers were out of business.

The railroads, once the pride and joy of American mass transportation, were crippled by the rise of commercial aviation, aided and abetted by the development of the jet engine. They have never recovered their former glory. As we've seen already, mechanical engineers in Rochester, New York, underestimated the impact of electronics in the 1970s and early 1980s, and it cost many of them their livelihood.

Even though you are back in employment, it is absolutely vital that you keep learning. There are always skills to be mastered and new knowledge to acquire. Today's worker needs always to develop fresh marketable proficiencies that will prevent him or her from becoming obsolete in the fast-changing workplace.

Using Your Gifts

Perhaps during this period of unemployment, you have noticed things about yourself that you want to develop. Not only would these fulfill you, but they might improve your ability to hold down your job, start a new business, or eventually move into a different, more challenging field full of fascinating opportunities. If you have, then explore the possibilities. Even if these explorations lead nowhere, at least you will not find yourself sometime in the future looking back in regret and wondering about what might have been.

We are stewards of the gifts and skills God has entrusted to us. Good stewards, rather than allowing their resources to molder, use them, upgrade them, and add to them through education. In so doing they are investing in their future.

Most of us would be horrified if our physicians failed to do continuing education. We want our doctors to understand new treatments that can help their patients—including us. If CPAs refused to stay abreast of the ever-changing tax laws, they could land us, their clients, in "deep doo-doo." Today all workers at the very least should keep themselves up-to-date with developments in their own field. Not only does this make us better at our jobs, but it also enables us to read the writing on the wall so we don't go the same way as buggy whip makers, or Rochester's mechanical engineers.

A friend of mine runs a small audio and video business. He actually holds a bachelor's degree in music, beginning life as a professional musician. This led into radio and television, and he spent much of his life working in broadcasting. Then a few years ago, when the company for which he worked got into trouble, he set out on his own. The mix of skills he has accumulated incrementally throughout his working life stood him in good stead, but with recording and video technology changing at the speed of light, he has had to work hard to keep up.

With more and more businesses needing video and audio resources for training their personnel, advertising, and so forth, he has found himself uniquely equipped to produce a low-cost, high quality product. He is now finding that his hobbies and professional past have started to merge and are making him a living. He is also evidence that no one is ever too old to learn new tricks, because as I write this he is about to celebrate his sixty-fifth birthday!

As you prepare to get back into the work force, perhaps you should take an audit of your strengths and weaknesses. With this inventory of your assets, you should look for ways to keep them in top condition. It might mean subscribing to—and then reading—additional professional journals. It might mean enrolling for evening classes or even studying for another degree. Take advantage of any continuing education your new employer offers. Not only will you make yourself better at your job, but by improving your skills you will actually make work much more fun as well. You may also soon discover there are exciting new facets of the world of work where you can specialize, develop much-needed skills, or have a special talent to exploit.

The worker who stays in a job in the twenty-first century will be a person who is a good steward of his or her abilities. To be a good steward means being a constant learner. I used my time out of work a decade ago finding out how a computer works. Desktop PCs were very new in those days, and few people had any idea how they functioned or what their value might be in the workplace. By laying the foundation of my computer skills at that particular time, I have been able to stay a whisker ahead of the game ever since, and have possibly saved my present organization thousands and thousands of dollars.

Your Résumé

Many people are tempted to abandon their résumé as soon as the job search is over. They breathe a sign of relief, stuff it in a file, and store it away in the darkest corner of their filing cabinet, hoping they will never have to stare the ugly thing in the face again. It has accompanied them everywhere for weeks—even months—and not having to worry about it any longer makes them feel like a prisoner being released from shackles!

But I have a word of caution: Despite the fact that you are going back to work, you never know when you will need your résumé again. Yes, you probably want to take a break from having to look that document in the eye, and the business of settling in a new job will certainly take up much of your time. But, for goodness' sake, don't forget it altogether. Bring it out and dust it off occasionally.

It is vital that you keep your résumé up-to-date. I have mine saved on my computer just in case I need it, and every few months I pull it up to review it. When a detail changes, I am able to update it right away. Occasionally, if I'm in a particularly creative mood, I pull the document to pieces and put it together in, what I hope, is a more effective way. I often do this after having looked over my journals. Time and again, as I glance back over the past, I realize I've done something that ought to be recorded in some way in that all-important document that outlines my career to date.

When I was invited to apply for the position that I knew was totally out of my league, overcome by vanity at being made part of that process, I filled in the forms and answered a seemingly endless catalogue of questions. Those questions were as exhaustive as any I have ever been asked. By the time I reached the end of the process, I had learned so much about myself that I knew the time had come to significantly rework my resume. Even if you're not interested in moving, occasionally applying for positions gives you an opportunity of testing yourself and your skills against the backdrop of today's market. It can also prove a good time to modify your résumé for the time when you will really need it.

In such a fluid job market, you have no idea when the possibility of another position is going to present itself. You may not know when your employer is going to change the whole format of the corporation—or downsize. Perhaps you can only guess how secure or "permanent" your present position is; what looks a certainty today may be gone tomorrow. Having a résumé tucked away in a quiet little subdirectory somewhere on your computer may be a precaution, like wearing both belt and suspenders, but it is a wise one.

Relocation

It might be that your new position requires you to move to another city. There is something very exciting about moving. In this instance, you really are starting over in many ways. But what amazes me is the number of people who think that relocation is the solution to all their problems. What is exciting can also be very painful.

Certainly, you are leaving behind some of the baggage from the past, but the wear and tear of relocation are higher than most of us realize. Moving is not so much escape from past errors; it is more like repositioning a shrub in your backyard. The hole in which you place it might be a better position for that particular piece of vegetation, but pulling up its roots is traumatic, to say the least!

133

I have moved more times than I care to count, including migrating across an ocean, so I know what I'm talking about when I say that relocation has hidden costs. For nearly a decade now, I have been living in a small town that sees a steady flow of families moving in for a few years while one spouse attends seminary, then moving on to someplace else. The thrill of a "fresh start" in a new place very quickly gives way to anxieties about children unable to settle into a new school, whether the spouse of the seminary student can find a job, and the real discomfort of losing those support systems that were so nicely in place in the family's old home.

Add to this the fact that as you get older, it becomes progressively more difficult to replace the supportive relationships you lose when you move on. My wife and I have a huge Christmas mailbag because we have acquaintances all over the world, but almost all our deepest friendships are with persons we got to know twenty or twenty-five years ago. The trouble is, they live in places like England, France, Tanzania, and Canada, nowhere near our home on the Cumberland Plateau in Tennessee.

A change of address brings a financial burden too. Perhaps the housing market is slow and you have trouble selling your home, or because property prices are so much higher in your new location, you are stretched to find something you can afford. Our neighbors of a few years ago moved from our town in rural Tennessee to the Virginia suburbs of Washington, D.C.—talk about sticker shock when they went to find a new home! And then there are always unexpected expenses of setting up housekeeping in a new environment.

Challenges, both financial and emotional, are there to be surmounted. A new position engenders fresh enthusiasm, so it is often much easier to tackle such difficulties than it might have been a few months earlier. At that time you were pouring all your psychological and spiritual energy into your career search. However, be careful not to bite off more than you can chew. It is unwise to make any more changes at once than is absolutely necessary.

It is also vital that you find emotional and spiritual support in your new community. If I were moving again, my first priority would be to find a church family where I could find the friendships that would give me the encouragement I need.

Some of our oldest friends belong to a congregation where one of my seminary classmates is pastor. We visited him and his wife recently, and finished up at a social gathering with a group of church people. I found myself drawn into conversation with a couple who had moved from a very different part of the country, hundreds of miles from family and friends. Settling down was difficult, made worse when one of their children was given a tough time at school. Christian people came to the rescue, and to their immense surprise this thoroughly secular pair found themselves being drawn not only into the church's fellowship, but also into a loving friendship with Jesus Christ.

Even if a relationship with the church is something new to you, it can be an "instant community" when we find ourselves attempting to put down roots in a new place, and Christian people always seem to have more in common with us than those differences that separate us from them. Perhaps it would be a good idea to find out something about all the churches in the neighborhood to which you are going before packing the moving van, so that you'll have an idea which one might suit you that very first weekend in your new home.

Happily Ever After . . . ?

Perhaps not, but then I'm not certain you would want life to be an endless stream of "happily ever afters." While I might rail against it at the time, and lie awake in the middle of the night worrying, I like the rich texture that joy and sorrow, hardship and ease seem to give to my life. I definitely don't appreciate what makes me miserable when I'm experiencing it, but when I can look back and see the beauty of its intricate pattern, I discover I have a lot to be thankful for.

The position I have held since my last tumultuous job search has been far from easy, and there have been times when I have thought that I was about to come to pieces. But in retrospect, I have been able to see that I was brought by God to a wonderful place for my daughters to grow to adulthood and my wife to find work that stretches and fulfills her. We are not without our disappointments and discouragements, but even in the hard times we have been given opportunities for growth and Christian service which would not have existed otherwise.

Of course, I have a list of complaints about my job and the place where I live, but these are burrs under the saddle with which we must learn to live when compared with the string of other blessings that have accompanied them. We certainly haven't lived "happily ever after," but after the most unsettling period of our lives, we have found ourselves able to move forward to sunnier uplands. Interestingly, many of the lessons learned during the time we were caught in the thickets of unemployment have been invaluable for our lives since then.

> *God is a great ecologist with our lives— never wasting anything! Even the very worst things that have happened to you can be turned from apparent devastation into something good, lovely, and beautiful, just as an oyster transforms an irritating piece of sand which drifts into its shell into the most fabulous pearl.*

I am a firm believer that God is a great ecologist with our lives—he never wastes anything! Even the very worst things that have happened to you can be turned by God from apparent devastation into something good, lovely, and beautiful, just as an oyster transforms an irritating grain of sand that drifts into its shell into the most fabulous pearl.

You now stand on the threshold of a new beginning, you are starting over. The experiences you have come through during the last few months have probably made you a wiser person, with more, not less, to share with society. Today's world needs people like you, and God can use you to make this aching planet a better place—if you will let him.

The General Thanksgiving

Almighty God, Father of all mercies,
we your unworthy servants give you humble thanks
for all your goodness and loving-kindness
to us and to all whom you have made.
We bless you for our creation, preservation,
and all the blessings of this life;
but above all for your immeasurable love
in the redemption of the world by our Lord Jesus Christ;
for the means of grace, and for the hope of glory.
And, we pray, give us such an awareness of your mercies,
that with truly thankful hearts we may show forth your
    praise,
not only with our lips, but in our lives,
by giving up our selves to your service,
and by walking before you
in holiness and righteousness all our days;
through Jesus Christ our Lord,
to whom, with you and the Holy Spirit,
be honor and glory throughout all ages. Amen.

A Gaelic Blessing

May the road rise up to meet you,
May the wind be always at your back,
May the sun lie warm upon your face,
The rains fall softly upon your fields,
And until we meet again,
May the Lord hold you in the hollow of His hand.

137

APPENDIX:
RESOURCES TO HELP YOU IN YOUR SEARCH

A successful job search is helped along by friends to support you, and sources of information to enable you to reach your objectives effectively. I commend to you the following books and ideas.

Job Hunt Books

Bolles, Richard. *What Color Is Your Parachute?* San Francisco: Ten Speed Press.

This is the job search classic of all times. Bolles, an Episcopal priest, updates it annually. I find the text a little tedious, but the appendices and other helps are masterly. His list of recommended reading, aids with résumés, etc., is outstanding. This is a must for everyone searching for a new position.

Richard Bolles has written various other books about job searches and life transitions. I would commend his short *The Quick Job-Hunting Map: A Fast Way to Help* and *The Three Boxes of Life*, both published by the Ten Speed Press.

Jackson, Tom. *Guerrilla Tactics in the Job Market.* New York: Bantam Books.

I think this is a much more readable book than *What Color Is Your Parachute?* It is informative, well-written, and helps you put the building-blocks of a job search together extremely well.

Mackay, Harvey. *Sharkproof*. New York: HarperCollins.

Personal prejudice got in the way when I started reading this book because I was determined not to like it. But the author of *Swim with the Sharks* and *Beware of the Naked Man Who Offers You His Shirt* offers an engaging view of the job search process. A successful businessperson, Mackay has his finger on the pulse of American commerce and knows what needs to be done if you are to make it. In *Sharkproof*, what he does is offer a portrait of a successful job hunt from the view of a potential employer.

Morton, Tom. *The Survivor's Guide to Unemployment*. Pinon Press.

A helpful book dealing with the nuts and bolts of surviving while you are between jobs. There is good information about the unemployment benefits you might qualify for, and practical suggestions about surviving the hardships that sometimes accompany unemployment. Growing out of Morton's experience of seventeen months without work, it attempts to show how you can maintain your integrity through hard times and mature as a person.

Publications

National Business Employment Weekly. Princeton, N.J.: Dow Jones and Company. Good articles, helpful guidance and insights, and loads of want ads and advertisements for national and international professional positions. While a priceless asset, it could be rather an expensive investment if you are having to watch your budget, but it might be something you could share with others. Available on newsstands, bookstore magazine racks, and through quarterly subscriptions. Address: NBEW, P. O. Box 300, Princeton, NJ 08543-0300. Phone: 609-520-4305. Fax: 609-520-4309.

Spiritual Helps

All sorts of aids and helps are available from Christian bookstores, church libraries, and the like. It is important that you find what suits you best. If you need help with this, talk to your pastor or other Christian leader.

Try giving daily Bible reading a prime place in your spiritual discipline. Good translations are the New International Version (NIV), the New Revised Standard Version (NRSV) and the more conversational Good News Bible—Today's English Version, published by the American Bible Society. These days you can also get a variety of Bible translations for your computer. I have been very happy with Parsons Software QuickVerse; not only is it available at a modest price, but also you can add different translations as needed.

If you have trouble getting started in daily Bible reading, try one of the daily devotionals many publishers provide. I like daily helps from The Upper Room (Nashville, TN), Scripture Union (Philadelphia, PA), Forward Movement (Cincinnati, OH), and the Bible Reading Fellowship (Orlando, FL). Personally, I use the notes from the Bible Reading Fellowship in England, which are available to the public in the United States through the Evangelical Education Society, 2300 9th St South, Arlington, VA 22204-2351; phone 703-521-2351.

There are all sorts of books of prayers and devotionals on the market, but I would recommend the *Book of Common Prayer* and Oswald Chambers's *My Utmost for His Highest*. If you are trying to develop a spiritual discipline in your life, then you might appreciate Richard Foster's *The Celebration of Discipline* (San Francisco: HarperCollins Religious). SPCK Publications of England produces many fine little books of prayers for personal use; details about these are available from Cokesbury's chain of Christian bookstores.

If you are trying to use a journal to help you grow spiritually, then you might consider looking at *At a Journal Workshop by Ira Progoff* (New York: Dialogue House Library) and *Adventure Inward*, by Morton T. Kelsey (Minneapolis: Augsburg-Fortress Press).

Counseling

If you need spiritual counseling, the place to start is with your pastor. He or she will be able to direct you to a therapist, if you need the kind of in-depth assistance that a parish pastor is not able to provide. Career counseling is a growing field, and there are some very helpful counselors around, but there are some who prey on vulnerable people in time of need. If you are looking for a career-counseling professional, check references and see if you can get to talk to some former clients.

APPENDIX

Support Groups

Local churches of all denominations sponsor groups for men and women who are in the midst of a career transition. Some churches offer groups especially for older job seekers. Sometimes these support groups are advertised, but more often news of them travels by word of mouth. *The National Business Employment Weekly* provides occasional information about Christian and Jewish congregations that provide a setting in which job searchers can explore the various possibilities.